THE MEANIN

DIRT

THE MEANING IS IN THE
DIRT

Meditations on Life's Richness

**Marlette B. Reed, BEd, MA &
Annette M. Lane, RN, PhD**

THE MEANING IS IN THE DIRT
Copyright © 2020 by Marlette B. Reed, BEd, MA
& Annette M. Lane, RN, PhD

Unless otherwise indicated, scripture taken from the Holy Bible, NEW INTERNATIONAL VERSION®, NIV® Copyright © 1973, 1978, 1984, 2011 by Biblica, Inc.® Used by permission. All rights reserved worldwide. Scripture quotations marked (NCV) are taken from the New Century Version®. Copyright © 2005 by Thomas Nelson. Used by permission. All rights reserved. Scripture quotations marked (MSG) are taken from The Message. Copyright © by Eugene H. Peterson 1993, 1994, 1995, 1996, 2000, 2001, 2002. Used by permission of NavPress Publishing Group. Scripture quotations marked (KJV) are taken from the Holy Bible, King James Version, which is in the public domain. Scripture quotations marked (GNT) are taken from the Good News Translation - Second Edition © 1992 by American Bible Society. Used by permission. Scripture quotations marked (MEV) are taken from the Modern English Version. Copyright © 2014 by Military Bible Association. Used by permission. All rights reserved. Scripture quotations marked (NLT) are taken from the Holy Bible, New Living Translation, copyright ©1996, 2004, 2007 by Tyndale House Foundation. Used by permission of Tyndale House Publishers, Inc., Carol Stream, Illinois 60188. All rights reserved. Scripture quotations marked (ERV) are taken from the Easy-to-Read Version of the Bible, Copyright © 2006 by Bible League international. Scripture quotations marked (NASB) are taken from the New American Standard Bible®, Copyright © 1960, 1962, 1963, 1968, 1971, 1972, 1973, 1975, 1977, 1995 by The Lockman Foundation. Used by permission. Scripture quotations marked (TLB) are taken from The Living Bible copyright © 1971 by Tyndale House Foundation. Used by permission of Tyndale House Publishers Inc., Carol Stream, Illinois 60188. All rights reserved. The Living Bible, TLB, and the The Living Bible logo are registered trademarks of Tyndale House Publishers. Scripture quotations marked (AMP) are taken from the Amplified® Bible, Copyright © 1954, 1958, 1962, 1964, 1965, 1987 by The Lockman Foundation. Used by permission. Scripture quotations marked (NLV) are taken from the *New Life Version*, copyright © 1969 and 2003. Used by permission of Barbour Publishing, Inc., Uhrichsville, Ohio 44683. All rights reserved.

Printed in Canada

Print ISBN: 978-1-4866-1895-8
eBook ISBN: 978-1-4866-1896-5

Word Alive Press
119 De Baets Street, Winnipeg, MB R2J 3R9
www.wordalivepress.ca

Cataloguing in Publication may be obtained through Library and Archives Canada

To Brian and Jon:
You two guys bring so much meaning to my life. Thank you!
(MBR)

To my husband, Dave:
Thanks for almost a quarter century of cherished marriage.
(AML)

CONTENTS

Section Four: Weeding

Section Five: The Harvest

INTRODUCTION

The seed for this book was planted during a time of great difficulty in our lives. Annette had been diagnosed with Stage Four cancer (her second bout of cancer in fourteen years). She'd undergone one surgery, was undergoing chemotherapy, and was looking toward another operation in the future. I (Marlette) wasn't ill with cancer, but at times I felt sick watching my beloved twin sister suffer. (I identified strongly with Annette's suffering. After struggling for over thirty years with rheumatoid arthritis, I related intensely to physical pain, emotional suffering, and the existential question, *What does the future hold?*)

Early in Annette's second bout of cancer, we were walking in a mall one Saturday, seeking to exercise carefully. Her cancer had metastasized to one of her hips, and we didn't want it to break! In the process of our laps, we talked about "sanitized lives"—lives that were neat and tidy but largely dull for those living them. In this sense, "cleanliness was *not* next to godliness" (to modify the old adage). Living lives without risk, without ever getting our hands dirty, perhaps without even having a pet (because they soil the carpet and then, when you're firmly attached to them, they die) can be devoid of meaning. We concluded that "the meaning is in the dirt!" Annette said, "That would make a great book title," and the seed of the plan we had talked about for years—to compose a book of short meditations—was planted.

This book is far more than musings on physical suffering. We each have lengthy careers working with people in progress. I was a teacher and now am a chaplain, including having worked for almost a decade with dying people in a hospice. Annette is a PhD-prepared nurse. She served a two-year stint in a war zone in the 1980s and a couple of years as a crisis counsellor in a large city. The privilege of working with people in vulnerable situations has impacted us deeply, and out of these experiences/learnings, we write with the conviction that *the meaning is really in the dirt.*

We have provided sixty-five meditations that are divided into five sections. The title of each section relates to the metaphor of the dirt, which will become a garden: "Preparing the Ground," "Tilling the Soil," "Planting," "Weeding," and "The Harvest." Within these sections, we discuss the importance of making meaning in our lives, character formation, the effort and discipline it takes to make meaning, adversity and difficulties in making meaning, and the impact of our meaning-making on society. On each section page, we list the specific meditations included in that section. This will allow you to quickly locate any meditation that piques your interest. Some topics contain several parts; the parts may follow sequentially or they may appear in different sections of the book, depending on where they best fit.

We hope this book affirms you in the ways you're making meaning in your life and the world; we also hope it provides the seeds for greater meaning, and that as you plant those seeds, you will reap a satisfying and influential harvest.

We'd like to thank Word Alive Press for working with us on this project. We're particularly grateful for the guidance, excellent suggestions, and professionalism of Tia Friesen. Her knowledge, coupled with her humour, has made this partnership a pleasure!

This book is written in a conversational manner. To avoid confusion, the pronoun "I" refers to Marlette. When Annette is speaking, this will be clearly identified.

Join us through these meditations on meaning, growth, and purpose—surprisingly nestled in the metaphor of *dirt*.

Marlette Reed
Annette Lane
August 2019

SECTION ONE
PREPARING THE GROUND

INTRO TO SECTION ONE

All gardeners at the beginning of their projects prepare the ground. This involves removing the rocks from the dirt and clarifying the dimensions of the garden-to-be through stakes in the ground. Can you imagine a gardener just scattering seed willy-nilly in an open space filled with rocks and thorns and, perhaps, garbage that has been blown in by the wind? Jesus considered this in the parable of the sower (Matthew 13). We begin this book by defining the parameters of the garden-to-be. We explain our metaphors and clearly state the assumptions under which we wrote our meditations.

1.1 The Meaning Is in the Dirt: "Dirt" Defined
1.2 The Meaning Is in the Dirt: The Metaphor Explained
1.3 Too Small for Me
1.4 Made for God
1.5 Vocation: Meaning in Us; Meaning for the World
1.6 What Is Success?

1.1 THE MEANING IS IN THE DIRT: "DIRT" DEFINED

What a strange title for a book. How on earth does meaning in life relate to dirt? (Yes, the pun is intended.) Merriam-Webster defines dirt as: "a soiling substance; loose or packed soil or sand; an abject or filthy state, squalor."[1] Depending upon the definition, dirt can be neutral or positive (soil—that from which our food grows), negative (something that makes one dirty), or the state of being foul or coarse.

Dirt can also make someone dirty but, in the proper context, produce something good. Gardeners and farmers know this well. The same manure that causes stains on our clothing and (perhaps) smells bad can also be excellent fertilizer for crops. As children, we often went to our beloved cousins' farm in the summer for a couple of weeks; as city girls, we laughed at the farm implement called a "manure spreader," but that piece of equipment made a significant difference in the growth of crops.

We use the term "dirt" in a variety of ways in this book of meditations. Dirt can make us dirty; it can represent human suffering; it can house death (decaying leaves, for example) but later bring forth life. It can also be the stuff of growth. With some work and co-operation with the Creator—our Master Gardener—it can produce good fruit in our lives (Galatians 5:22–23).

---

1   *Merriam-Webster Dictionary*, s.v. "Dirt," accessed: June 1, 2019, https://www.merriam-webster.com/dictionary/dirt.

In a few places in this book, we refer to dirt in the purely negative sense. Dirt from which nothing good can come. In these cases, we clearly state that "the meaning is *not* in the dirt," and we encourage readers to get out of the dirt pile.

Who knew that there was so much meaning hidden in the word "dirt"?

1.2 THE MEANING IS IN THE DIRT: THE METAPHOR EXPLAINED

In the previous meditation, we looked at the qualities of dirt. Now we move deeper into the explanation of our metaphor. What is meaning in life? Is it having a life of fun or reading ancient philosophers? Or perhaps it involves listening to music that moves the soul? While there can be meaning in these experiences, a rich life requires more.

We live in a society of contradictions. On the one hand, our culture runs people ragged, but on the other hand, it promotes ease (with so many labour-saving devices). In some ways, society provides opportunities for relationship (technology that enables instantaneous communication), but in other ways, people have never been more isolated and lonely (many do not even know their neighbours). Incidental meaning is often absent, and people in twenty-first-century North America need to make concerted efforts at building richness into life.

Doing the inner work of the soul can be messy; this is the development of character and holiness that's required to become mature. Hence, we have devoted Section Two to *being* and *becoming*. Sustained meaning in life comes through character; the immature soul lacks the character to persevere and co-operate with the Holy Spirit in doing the work that brings great richness.

Making meaning takes effort, requiring both discipline and spiritual disciplines (Section Three).[2] Working with people in difficult circumstances, such as homelessness, isn't easy. It requires us to learn how to knowledgeably help. In these situations, learning goes beyond simply acquiring a body of knowledge; rather, it entails *being*—learning to be comfortable responding to those who may be different from us or in strenuous circumstances. The outer work of life can get our hands dirty. As lovely as it can be to have a pet, cleaning up after them is not!

In Section Four, we examine dealing with adversities and difficulties. These can be impediments to meaning; surprisingly, some of the deepest richness in life can come through these experiences. Our response to adversity is important, so we'll present ways of responding to and growing through difficulties.

Finally, making an impact in this world is meaningful (Section Five). That purposefulness is life-affirming to those we impact and to ourselves. While being involved in causes and with people is stretching, it's also growth-producing. "It feeds me," said one woman about her volunteer work in a nursing home. This is also a part of our Creator's master plan—that we would be given the privilege of impactful work and living. As the Apostle Paul stated, *"For we are God's handiwork, created in Christ Jesus to do good works, which God prepared in advance for us to do"* (Ephesians 2:10).

---

2   See A.M. Lane and M.B. Reed, *Making Meaning in Older Age: Bringing Together the Pieces of Your Life,* (Winnipeg, MB: Word Alive Press, 2017).

1.3 TOO SMALL FOR ME

To bless is to put a bit of yourself into something.
It is to make holy, to change something or someone
because of your presence.[3]

—Macrina Wiederkehr

Though it sounds like a contradiction in terms, I truly am
too small for me, and you are too small for you! We can't
be the centre of our own universes and find lasting meaning.
Many people seek to find purpose, be happy, and leave a legacy
by pursuing their own interests, hobbies, and passions. Unless
those pursuits positively impact others, it's unlikely these activities will bring richness over the long haul. Many people in
their last days feel like they "missed it," because they come to
understand too late that connection—to others and to God—is
at the heart of life's purpose. We've been created to live in relation with others and to bless them.

The opening quotation speaks of the changes we can
bring into situations and other people by our presence, our input, our very selves. Through this giving, we are strengthened,
changed, and blessed. Our selflessness makes others holy by
honouring the image of God within them and by bringing light

---

3   "The Almond Tree." *The Sacred Braid*. Accessed March 20, 2019. https://
www.thesacredbraid.com/2017/02/20/life-line-55/.

and life into dark situations. It works the other way around too: we're blessed also as we're changed in the process of being change agents. We are made holier (but not holier-than-thou).

If you lack meaning in your day-to-day life, it may be because your focus has been too small. To understand that we're too small for ourselves isn't demeaning; rather, it suggests the need for a larger focus. Cast your bread upon the water—there will be a return (see Ecclesiastes 11:1). We trust that you and those you impact will be blessed as you "make holy, change someone because of your presence."[4]

---

4 Ibid.

1.4 MADE FOR GOD

You have made us for yourself, O Lord, and our heart is restless until it rests in you.[5]

—St. Augustine

I am "too small for me." I was made for much more; I was made for God. Along with the teachings of the scriptures, we're surrounded by evidence that human beings are made for God. This evidence includes our need to worship, our sense of connection to God when we're in nature, and the soul's restlessness despite "having it all" (material goods).

The need to worship is seen in childhood. Children love to admire and emulate sports heroes or celebrities. Even in adulthood, individuals "follow" Hollywood stars. They even change hair and clothing styles to copy the famous.

The vastness of nature also draws us to God. Perhaps it's a physical representation of the transcendent—what was here long before us and what will remain after we're gone (the mountains, for example).

---

5   St. Augustine, *Confessions* (trans. R.S. Pine-Coffin), (NY: Penguin Books, 1961), 21.

Material wealth doesn't guarantee happiness. While North Americans are wealthy compared to much of the world, increasing suicide rates would suggest that we're not happy.[6]

What does it mean to be made for God? Our Creator made us in His image (Genesis 1:26–27); He knows what will fill us, what will give our lives meaning. In the Bible He provides many clues to how to live meaningfully. For example, Jesus masterfully explains about the soil from which all the commandments have root, often referred to as the two greatest commandments. Besides loving Him with all that we are, He directs us to love others as ourselves (Matthew 22:36-40). Between the two commandments, Jesus adds this explanation: *"and the second is like* [the first]" (v. 39). We demonstrate our love for God by loving others, so by loving others, we find meaning.

We look to Him in worship, recognizing Him for who He is; we appreciate the world He has made (nature and humanity), and we live in the way He asks us to live. Early in his life, King Solomon was renowned for his wisdom; however, later he lost his focus and tried everything life had to offer. He played in dirt piles that he shouldn't have been in; rather than being happy, he found his experiences to be "meaningless" (Ecclesiastes 1:2). Toward the end of his life, he reached the following conclusion: *"Honor God and obey his commands, because this is all people must do"* (Ecclesiastes 12:13, NCV).

Jesus said, *"Take my yoke upon you and learn from me, for I am gentle and humble in heart, and you will find rest for your souls. For my yoke is easy and my burden is light"* (Matthew 11:29–30). Our rest and meaning are found in the One who made us and loves us.

---

6   "Suicide Rates Increasing Across America." *Centers for Disease Control and Prevention.* Accessed June 7, 2018 https://www.cdc.gov/media/releases/2018/p0607-suicide-prevention.html.

1.5 VOCATION: MEANING IN US; MEANING FOR THE WORLD

In setting out the stakes of this garden of meaning, we also want to address the idea of "calling" or "vocation." Do some people have a calling while others do not?

First, we should clarify these synonyms. The Merriam-Webster thesaurus provides synonyms for vocation, including "work, occupation, lifework."[7] While these can be elements of vocation, the terms "vocation" and "calling" are often used in a much deeper sense.

Micah 6:8 indicates a broad calling that applies to each one of us—a way of living that's paraphrased beautifully by Eugene Peterson in *The Message*:

> But he's already made it plain how to live, what to do, what God is looking for in men and women. It's quite simple: Do what is fair and just to your neighbor, be compassionate and loyal in your love, And don't take yourself too seriously—take God seriously.

How different our society would be if everyone took this as their calling!

---

7   *Merriam-Webster Thesaurus*, s.v. "Vocation," accessed July 17, 2019, https://www.merriam-webster.com/thesaurus/vocation.

There's also a personal calling that fits the way the Creator designed each individual. This type of vocation can involve paid or unpaid work/effort but reflects the image of God within that person. It reflects God's character in each person, their personality and what brings them joy in making this world a better place.

We love Frederick Buechner's definition of calling. He refers to it as "the place where your deep gladness meets the world's deep need."[8] How wonderful that vocation is meant to be joyful! Contrary to what people often think, calling is not exclusively a religious vocation; rather, it refers to contributions to the *world*, not simply to or through the organized church. The person whose "deep gladness meets the world's deep need" may be doing this in a myriad of ways: through their personality, through their gifts and passions, or through their resources.

One dear lady, "Sally," said to me, "I'm seventy-five years old, and I still don't know what I was put here to do!" Part of the answer to her existential angst is that she didn't regard her beautiful gifts as being important (I affirmed that they are). But another aspect to this common statement of soul pain is that, in our society, we often don't listen to our lives. As you move through subsequent sections of this book, listen to your heart and your soul as to what moves you. This small book of meditations may identify an aspect of your calling and encourage you in your use and development of it, increasing your meaning and the meaning others experience through you. Or it may unlock some forgotten or unrealized aspects of your vocation, perhaps encouraging you to pursue them.

8   Frederick Buechner, *Wishful Thinking: A Seeker's ABC* (San Francisco, CA: HarperOne, 1993), 119.

What Is Success?

1.6 WHAT IS SUCCESS?

As we continue to stake out the boundaries of the dirt pile that will become your garden, it's important to consider the metrics of how success is defined. Success is broadly discussed in various arenas, such as books, television, and church, but how it's conceptualized differs. What does "success" mean? For some people, success involves attaining a high level of education and working in a highly rated profession. Others view success as achieving a very large bank account and accumulating valued material goods, such as real estate and "toys" like flashy cars and boats. ("Whoever has the most toys at the end of life wins!" states one bumper sticker.) Serving others as well as God constitutes success for some.

It's important to understand how we define success, not only in terms of our training and activities, but also our souls. It may help us appreciate why we may be making a lot of money but feel strangely dissatisfied. While our minds tell us that we're doing a good job and contributing to society (which may very well be true), our souls are restless because our work isn't meaningful to who we are as individuals.

We can respond in different ways to the dissonance between our experience and our souls. We may decide to more clearly stake out our boundaries of what's important and what's not. Some may continue to work in their current positions but volunteer for organizations that address causes

13

they feel strongly about, particularly if their income is needed to sustain the family. Others may give significant amounts of money to their favourite organizations, or volunteer in short term projects overseas to build schools or churches. Volunteer commitments to support worthwhile causes may add great meaning to individuals' lives. For others, volunteer work isn't satisfying enough, so they may change careers. This may occur at the height of one's career, or it may prompt retirement in their fifties or sixties, with subsequent retraining for different employment.

Defining what success means for you and how you wish to increase congruence between your time/activities and your values is important. Your own meaning-making depends on it.

It had long since come to my attention that people of accomplishment rarely sat back and let things happen to them. They went out and happened to things.[9]

—Leonardo da Vinci

---

9   "Success Quotes." *Goodreads*. Accessed August 8, 2019. https://www.goodreads.com/quotes/tag/success?page=2.

SECTION TWO
TILLING THE SOIL

Intro to Section Two

Having set the stakes for the proposed garden, we need to prepare the soil to receive seeds. *Tilling* involves preparing the ground to give access to water, air, and nutrients deep in the soil, where the plants will have access to them. One can introduce larger amounts of organic material into a garden that has been tilled, which will help the crops grow. Finally, tilling breaks up crusty pieces of soil into finer particles, allowing roots and root vegetables room to spread out.

This is the deep work of preparing to plant. Revisiting our metaphor: tilling refers to the work on a person's character to produce personality traits that allow for good growth. It's often unseen (below the ground), sometimes painful (Breaking up the crustiness of our character flaws can hurt!), and can, by introducing humus (decayed plant and animal matter), develop life (humility) through death. This unseen work is vital to producing a healthy crop; without good soil, the crop likely won't last the season (Matthew 13). Wise is the individual who allows for the work of the Holy Spirit within their life and co-operates with God, the Master Gardener of our lives, so that the fruit born can be plentiful.

2.1 LOVE: THE FOUNDATION FOR RICHNESS

Love is patient, love is kind ... It does not dishonor others, it is not self-seeking, it is not easily angered ... It always protects, always trusts, always hopes, always perseveres. Love never fails.

—1 Corinthians 13:4–8a

L ove is an essential characteristic of tilling the soil and is crucial in all phases of working in the dirt of making meaning. Love is the foundation of richness in life.

Much has been said about love in songs, movies, and literature. Typically, the love spoken of refers to romantic love and is mainly about experience and enjoyment. The love put forward in popular songs or movies isn't the type of love necessary for making meaning. As noted in 1 Corinthians 13:4–8, love is not self-seeking but involves commitment over time (notice use of the word "always").[10] Commitment, as the foundation for mature love, is necessary to sustain making meaning over time. Consider the commitment demonstrated by parents of a child with a developmental disability, such as Down Syndrome. The tender care of their child doesn't end at eighteen years of age; it continues for many years, often into the

---

10   Please note that this does not mean that those engaging in making meaning should condone or stay in situations of abuse or violence.

parents' later years, until they're physically unable to continue their ministrations.

Perseverance, another quality of biblical love, continues even when parents can no longer provide physical care for their beloved adult child. When their child enters a group home or a long-term care facility, these parents regularly visit. They advocate for their adult child, bridging the transition between home and facility. They work to inform staff about the needs and preferences of their child and about effective approaches in relationship-building with them.

Most parents-to-be don't envision raising a child with a significant developmental disability when they learn that they're expecting, yet those who embrace this role may experience tremendous meaning and purpose. Their *capacity to* love and their *experience of* love grow tremendously. One caregiver of an adult with a developmental disability said, "I found love!"

When working with older adults, we've never heard a dying person say that they regretted not having made more money or attaining a higher social status. What we've heard is regret over how they'd invested their life: "I wish I had gotten married and had children," or "I wish I had put more energy into friendships." These are the regrets of having not spent more of their lives in exercising a love that involved commitment and perseverance.

I must trust that the little bit of love that I sow now will bear many fruits, here in this world and the life to come.[11]

—Henri Nouwen

11   "Love." *BrainyQuote*. Accessed: July 24, 2019. https://www.brainyquote.com/quotes/henri_nouwen_588351?src=t_love.

2.2 HUMILITY: LIFE THROUGH DEATH

Humility is a vital character trait of one who wishes to live a rich life. As many religious and non-religious sources have pointed out, the words "humility" and "humus" are related; the Latin root that translates as "earth" is the word from which we get the words humus and humility.[12] Humus is a black or brown material in the soil, a result of partially decomposed plant or animal material in the earth;[13] "fertilizer" is a synonym for humus. Humility is defined as the absence of arrogance;[14] "down-to-earthness" is one of its synonyms.

Let's unearth this. Healthy growth in a garden is greatly aided by broken down plant and animal materials—humus—which bring greater life, or the crop. Humility is also a function of reduction; in reduction, greater life may come from an individual.

To be clear, humility is not a feeling of worthlessness. The reduction produces a down-to-earthness that puts us on equal footing with all humanity; it's a process of realization that

---

12 Typing these two words together into a search engine will yield a number of results.

13 *Merriam-Webster Online Dictionary*, s.v. "Humus," accessed July 27, 2019, https://www.merriam-webster.com/dictionary/humus.

14 *Merriam-Webster Online Dictionary*, s.v. "Humility," accessed: July 27, 2019, https://www.merriam-webster.com/dictionary/humility.

brings us into proper estimation of ourselves and others. As Maya Angelou said, "While I know myself as a creation of God, I am also obligated to realize and remember that everyone else ... [is] also God's creation."[15] I am of inestimable worth, and so is everyone else (see Psalm 139:13–14). This realization changes how we view and treat others. It frees us from comparison and enables us to love others as we love ourselves (Matthew 22:36-40). "Humility is not thinking less of yourself, it's thinking of yourself less."[16]

Why is arrogance such a big deal? Proverbs declares, *"Pride goes before destruction, and a haughty spirit before a fall"* (16:18). Pride produces within a person a sense of superiority and sometimes a belief that the standards of living don't apply to them. The proud person will break rules, and sometimes the spirits of others, with their nose-in-the-air living. This may produce a sense of power, but ultimately it's isolating. A meaningful life is predicated upon connection, and humility tills the soil for richness in relationships with God and others, and in work and life. We who would gain our lives must lose them, Jesus taught (Matthew 16:25). "Losing" refers to the relinquishing, the death of false aspects of personality (such as a sense of superiority), so that we may dignify and help others; in this there is profound meaning for both the helper and the one being helped. Humility, like humus, produces life through death.

---

15 "Maya Angelou Quotes." *BrainyQuote.* Accessed July 27, 2019. https://www.brainyquote.com/quotes/maya_angelou_167463.

16 "C.S. Lewis Quotes." *Goodreads.* Accessed July 27, 2019. https://www.goodreads.com/quotes/7288468-humility-is-not-thinking-less-of-yourself-it-s-thinking-of.

2.3 EMPATHY ESSENTIAL!

In this day of self-obsession, we're in dire need of empathy. For the one who wants a meaningful life through helping others, empathy is a crucial character trait. What is empathy? Described simply, empathy is *your* pain in *my* heart; it's the ability to feel for and with another person. Synonyms include "understanding, mercifulness, tenderness."[17] Though "sympathy" is also listed as a synonym,[18] we agree with social worker Brené Brown's understanding that sympathy has an element of condescension in it, while empathy does not.[19] Who is in the best position to tell the difference between empathy and sympathy? The one on the receiving end!

Empathy emerges early in personality development and is initially modelled by key persons in a child's life. The growing child will see that his parents, teachers, neighbours, and coaches treat others with respect and care. These important others also teach empathy directly. When a child mistreats another child, or perhaps the dog, a caring adult will say words

---

17 *Merriam-Webster Thesaurus*, s.v. "Empathy," accessed August 7, 2019, https://www.merriam-webster.com/thesaurus/empathy.

18 Ibid.

19 The RSA. "Brené Brown on Empathy." YouTube video, 2:53. Posted [December 10, 2013]. https://www.bing.com/videos/search?q=Brene+Brown+-+youtube+-+empathy&view=detail&mid=40548622B1834D85D1D440548622B1834D85D1D4&FORM=VIRE.

such as "How would *you* feel if you were treated this way?" This helps a child to "put themselves in another's shoes."[20] For some children, modelling and gentle coaching are enough to produce this ability to feel for others. Some children need a little more help, such as consequences for their actions. Here again, the trusted others will mete out meaningful consequences to children who demonstrate a lack of empathy; these consequences are particular to an offense and are verbally connected to that offense. They are also appropriate to the action committed. In this, a child learns that while they are important in this world, so are others. This prepares a child to live in community.

Empathy is essential to relationship and a meaningful life. It not only keeps individuals from harming others but allows them to care deeply and be cared for deeply. The one who can *"Rejoice with those who rejoice; mourn with those who mourn"* (Romans 12:15) can be meaningfully helped when in need. They can also connect with their Saviour, the suffering servant of Isaiah 53, because they can be moved by the suffering of the Other.

If you believe that you lack empathy, there are ways to develop it in adulthood. Please see our second meditation on this topic found in Section Three of this book.

> ... *if [Christ's] love has made any difference in your life ... if you have a heart, if you care ... love each other. .. Don't push your way to the front ... Don't be obsessed with getting your own advantage ...*
> —Philippians 2:1–4 (MSG)

20　*The Free Dictionary,* s.v. "Idioms," accessed August 7, 2019, https://idioms.thefreedictionary.com/put+yourself+in+their+shoes.

2.4 INTEGRITY: MORE THAN HONESTY

Remember the days when business deals could be sealed with a handshake? Remember the saying, "A man's word is his bond"? Remember when children could leave their bikes on the lawn overnight and not worry that they'd be stolen? It may seem like a long time ago, but we remember those days. Honesty was a virtue and was actively taught in the home, in faith settings, and in the educational system. We judged a life by, and society functioned through, integrity.

Did you know that there's a deeper meaning to this word? Integrity also means "completeness, wholeness, incorruptibility, soundness, and undividedness."[21] While we often understand integrity to be actions of honesty (and it is), we sometimes forget that it's an internal state of being. A person of integrity doesn't compartmentalize sections of their life that they need to hide—dirt piles they shouldn't be playing in. Instead, they seek help for areas of the soul that need healing. They don't cover up their behaviour; they don't rationalize lies. One's personality is whole, not divided or dis-integrated (there's the word again, just in a slightly different form). "What you see is what you get."

---

21 *Merriam-Webster Dictionary*, s.v. "Integrity," accessed August 11, 2019, https://www.merriam-webster.com/dictionary/integrity.

This is the type of integrity that King David refers to in Psalm 51:6 when he spoke of what God desires: "*Behold, thou desirest truth in the inward parts: and in the hidden part thou shalt make me to know wisdom*" (KJV). *The Message* renders the verse this way: "*What you're after is truth from the inside out. Enter me, then; conceive a new, true life.*" Inner truth leads to outer actions of honesty, courage, and love.

How does this concept interact with meaning-making? First, the very desire for this type of character is God-honouring and brings meaning. We can know that God is working with us to "*conceive a new, true life.*" Second, honesty in life saves much sorrow. The person who lives a divided life, dishonestly and in corruption, incurs much stress! "A clear conscience means you can lay your head down on your pillow and sleep at night," our mom used to say. Third, integrity in our lives enables us to connect meaningfully with others and to sustain relationships. One can sustain employment and volunteer work because they can be trusted.[22]

Finally, the type of inner integrity God desires allows Him to work deeply within each person's heart. The One who is the truth will work in you "*to help you want to do and be able to do what pleases him*" (Philippians 2:13, NCV). This means deeper connection with God, greater conformity to the image of Christ, and the receiving of the gift of His work, His calling for you within the world. The upshot of integrity—inner wholeness—is meaning.

---

22   We say this recognizing that sometimes one loses a job or a promotion *because* of their integrity.

2.5 COURAGE (PART ONE): STAND UP AND BE COUNTED

"... be courageous; be strong."

—1 Corinthians 16:13b

We often view courage as a characteristic that one either possesses or fails to possess. If we follow this line of thinking, we may be tempted to envy those who appear fearless, as well as feel that we were short-changed when it came to the doling out of this quality. We may also neglect making tough decisions in our lives, believing that we haven't been given the stuff to deal with hard circumstances or choices.

Viewing courage as a personality characteristic that one either has or doesn't have is too simplistic a view. First, courage doesn't mean not feeling fearful; rather, as noted by Mark Twain, "Courage is resistance to fear, mastery of fear—not absence of fear."[23] Those who have courage feel the distress of fear but fight through it as they act in response to the challenge or threat.

Second, we need courage in our daily lives not just for big events, like running into a burning building to save a child, but also for less dramatic feats, like going to work every day when we dislike our jobs or our colleagues. It's a dogged grittiness

---

23   "Courage Quotes." *Goodreads*. Accessed June 6, 2019. https://www.goodreads.com/quotes/tag/courage.

that puts one foot in front of the other, continuing to give our best when it's not rewarded.[24] Perseverance takes courage and develops it.

This leads us into another type of valour—moral courage. To do what is right, to speak the truth when the situation demands it, to refuse to lie when the group is going in that direction, to engage in civil disobedience when necessary—this is ethical integrity. Rosa Parks, a hero of the civil rights movement in the United States in the 1960s, did this by refusing to sit in the back of the bus. Others act as "whistle-blowers" when the organizations with which they work behave unethically. These individuals make sacrifices to stand for what is right, and sometimes they lose their jobs and/or careers doing so.

How is courage fertile soil for meaning? Self-respect, earned through courage, is essential to soul satisfaction. Whether it's the courage to keep going, the courage to act in dangerous situations, or the courage to take a stand morally, courage develops character (Romans 5:3–5), which produces meaning. The late actress Mary Tyler Moore said, "You can't be brave if you've only had wonderful things happen to you."[25]

---

24 Sometimes one leaves a poor work situation in favour of a better one. But life can necessitate staying put when no solution is immediately apparent and bills need to be paid.

25 "Mary Tyler Moore Quotes." *BrainyQuote*. Accessed June 6, 2019. https://www.brainyquote.com/quotes/mary_tyler_moore_131899.

2.6 COURAGE (PART TWO): A LION'S HEART—THE INNER LIFE OF THE DISCIPLE

For this very reason, make every effort to add to your faith goodness; and to goodness, knowledge; and to knowledge, self-control; and to self-control, perseverance; and to perseverance, godliness; and to godliness, mutual affection; and to mutual affection, love. For if you possess these qualities in increasing measure, they will keep you from being ineffective and unproductive in your knowledge of our Lord Jesus Christ.

—2 Peter 1:5–8

There's a form of courage that's not widely understood or practiced. It involves both the work of God in a person's life and the individual's determination to co-operate with God's purposes. It's exercised through faith. What is this type of courage? It's the lion-heart of a follower of Christ. The Apostle Peter speaks of rigorous discipleship—making *every* effort to continue to add to our initial faith a list of challenging characteristics: goodness, knowledge, self-control, and so on.

Why do we struggle to live as disciples as the scriptures instruct? Perhaps we don't see Jesus in the grittiness of our lives. Our Jesus may be "sanitized." We may view Him like the picture in the church foyer: the Saviour with every hair in place, looking very pious and rather detached. Does He even see us in our Monday to Saturday lives? Perhaps we're not convinced that the inner life matters. All religions have codes of conduct; maybe we assume that outer actions equate to inner character.

Putting this passage of scripture into the context of the dirt of our lives, what do we do when we have been deeply wronged, suffered terrible loss, or have anguished over long-term unanswered prayer? These experiences often lead to bitterness toward life, others, and God. And understandably so. However, the call of Christ to the disciple—to make *every* effort to add, trusting that He will do what we cannot do—takes a lion's heart and the courage to believe that He sees, He knows, He understands, and that He, the Master Gardener, is at work within us and our circumstances.

Remember the disciples of Jesus in the boat during a night-time storm on the sea? They were far from shore, the waves were treacherous, and they were alone. When they saw Jesus walking toward them on the water they were (unsurprisingly) terrified! Jesus said to them, as He says to us in our circumstances, *"Take courage. It is I. Don't be afraid"* (Matthew 14:27).

2.7 STRENGTH AND TENDERNESS (PART ONE): AN UNBEATABLE PAIR

Strength and tenderness are two vital character traits for making meaning. Rather than acting in isolation, they work together when tilling the soil. Strength involves the ability to produce an effect.[26] This seems self-evident; however, some individuals remain mired in a state of ennui, of lethargy, where they do not or cannot exert themselves. More common are the individuals who, in their attempt to make meaning through helping others, *forcefully tell* others what they should do and feel! For example, when helping individuals who are mourning, coming into their home and telling them how they should feel and what they should do is generally not helpful!

Like strength, tenderness (a synonym of which is "compassion")[27] on its own may not be effective. Some individuals, through their great sensitivity, will support others even when those individuals resist accessing professional support or taking the necessary steps to help themselves. While well-intended, this tenderness may not be effective in moving others toward necessary change.

---

26 *Merriam-Webster Dictionary*, s.v. "Strength," accessed July 22, 2019, https://www.merriam-webster.com/dictionary/strength#synonyms.

27 *Merriam-Webster Thesaurus*, s.v. "Tenderness," accessed July 26, 2019, https://www.merriam-webster.com/thesaurus/tenderness.

Strength and tenderness acting in concert with each other forge a valuable approach to making meaning. Tenderness facilitates active listening to others, as well as sensitivity in allowing others to tell their stories. Strength helps us bear the stories (stories of trauma can be difficult to listen to) and, at a certain point, carefully begin to make some suggestions to others that may help them. Tenderness, however, tempers how we make suggestions, making us keenly aware of timing.[28]

Making meaning is challenging because of the characteristics necessary to effectively work with others. As we develop these traits, our effectiveness increases, and we ourselves are changed for the better. Listen to the Apostle Paul speak of the fruits of the Spirit that develop in the lives of believers who are in step with Him:

> *But what happens when we live God's way? He brings gifts into our lives, much the same way that fruit appears in an orchard—things like affection for others, exuberance about life, serenity. We develop a willingness to stick with things, a sense of compassion in the heart, and a conviction that a basic holiness permeates things and people. We find ourselves involved in loyal commitments, not needing to force our way in life, able to marshal and direct our energies wisely.*
> —Galatians 5:22–23 (MSG)

Do you see the unbeatable pairing of strength and tenderness in these verses?

---

28   Sometimes a more assertive approach is needed. For instance, if a person is actively suicidal and refuses to go to the hospital for an assessment, calling emergency services (police and ambulance) is appropriate.

2.8 Strength and Tenderness (Part Two): Revealed through Tears

There is a sacredness in tears. They are not the mark of weakness, but of power. They speak more eloquently than ten thousand tongues. They are the messengers of overwhelming grief, of deep contrition, and of unspeakable love.[29]

—Washington Irving

Some people are very uncomfortable with tears—their own, as well as the tears of others. Behind this discomfort may be their family of origin's admonishment that "Big boys (and girls) don't cry." But sincere tears (omitting the kind that are used to manipulate) reveal character.

As noted by Washington Irving, tears evidence and communicate caring. When we grieve, feel remorse, or love deeply, they show that we have the capacity to connect and feel disconnection. A tender person is safe—to themselves and to others.

Tears are also a sign of strength. The individual who can cry in front of others reveals strength through vulnerability. This individual is in touch with how they feel and has a strong enough self-esteem to allow others to witness and respond to their emotion. This is the power to which Irving attests.

---

29 "Washington Irving Quotes." *AZ Quotes*. Accessed June 03, 2019. https://www.azquotes.com/author/7202-Washington_Irving.

The ability to cry is necessary for joyful living. To experience the depth of emotion that brings tears allows us to experience the heights of emotion—hilarity, joy! It's understandable why we try to mute sadness or anger through preventing tears and blocking memories—the dirt of life has caused pain. Though dulling oneself in order to not feel so deeply, and therefore not cry, may achieve its desired effect, this blunting of emotion also quells roaring laughter and great happiness. As former Israeli Prime Minister Golda Meir aptly noted, "Those who do not know how to weep with their whole heart don't know how to laugh, either."[30]

If you doubt Irving's statement that tears are sacred, let us remind you of the shortest verse in the Bible: *"Jesus wept"* (John 11:35). Jesus's dear friend, Lazarus, had died. Those present at the tomb felt that Jesus wept because of His love for Lazarus (11:36). Indeed. But likely his tears were also for the crushing grief of the sisters of Lazarus, Mary and Martha, who were also Jesus's friends. And perhaps those tears were also for a world in which death is present—the "groaning creation" (Romans 8:22). Jesus wept because He tenderly cared; He loved; He grieved. Our tears bear witness to the image of God within us.

SECTION THREE
PLANTING

Intro to Section Three

An abandoned plot of land produces a number of things: remnants of the farmer's crops from days gone by, weeds, and other plants and flowers whose seeds happened to blow into that field. While it may look nice (or not), it doesn't reflect the desire of the farmer/gardener. If we wish to reap a desired harvest in our lives, we need to plant intentionally, carefully, and methodically. For example, it's not effective to dump all one's carrot seeds into a singular hole and expect many neat rows of carrots as well as beans and potatoes. We need knowledge, discipline, and effort—not just in one area but in a variety of areas—to plant effectively. Our gardening practices and life disciplines should nurture what is good and protect from what is not.

The next section of our book lays out many ways in which a person can plant, exert effort, and practice discipline in order to reap a later harvest of good, healthy crops. This section is intentionally longer than other parts of the book, as there are many ways to exert effort and practice discipline(s) that will regularly produce a meaningful crop.

3.1 GETTING OUR HANDS DIRTY THROUGH CREATIVITY

The soul of the artist cannot remain hidden.[31]

—Henri Nouwen

Creativity takes courage.[32]

—Henri Matisse

Creativity is a way in which individuals express their spirituality. An artist such as a sculptor, a painter, or a writer creates work that reflects their soul, passions, and ideas. For some, the meaningful work of creating draws them closer to God, the Creator of all creators.

More than simply getting their hands dirty in the elements of their craft, for many artists, creation is one way in which they work through difficult emotions or situations. While absorbed in their creative processes, artists can temporarily escape their internal pain, or perhaps work through some of it. As noted by the late priest and scholar, Henri Nouwen, an artist's soul is revealed within his or her work. This soul may include the artist's

---

31 "Henri J.M. Nouwen Quotes." *Goodreads.* Accessed June 16, 2019. https://www.goodreads.com/author/quotes/4837.Henri_J_M_Nouwen?page=2.

32 Creativity Quotes—Henri Matisse." *Goodreads.* Accessed June 16, 2019. https://www.goodreads.com/quotes/tag/creativity?page=1.

angst. For instance, within his writings, Nouwen wrote about vulnerability and loneliness. He bared his soul. It could be that writing was very therapeutic for him. Writing—creating with words through the dirt of life—brought forth beauty. Many have benefited from *The Wounded Healer*[33] and his other books.

There is, however, a danger in exposing one's soul through creativity. Others may not appreciate the work and may be critical. This may be why French artist Henri Matisse stated that it takes courage to be creative. Exposing the soul through creativity can leave artists feeling vulnerable or metaphorically naked. Hence many artists don't show or sell their work, as people's disinterest would be too painful. Some become famous, but posthumously. Few artists and authors can make a living through their work.

Nevertheless, the value of creative expression, if only to the artist, is significant. In Section Four, we examine "Spacious Lives" (Part Two), dealing with our inner world (you may wish to have a look at that meditation after this one). There we consider the importance of quietness and listening to one's soul. The artist can do that through the exercise (dare we say *discipline*) of creativity. In a society that is glued to time, the one focused on their craft may lose track of hours and minutes. They may hear their inner voice expressed through thoughts, shapes, or strokes of the brush. King David, the famous warrior king of Israel, was also an accomplished musician and poet. The *"man after* [God's] *own heart"* (Acts 13:22) expressed *his* heart back to God in ways we still find meaningful thousands of years later.

---

33   See Henri J.M. Nouwen, *The Wounded Healer: Ministry in Contemporary Society* (New York, NY: Doubleday, 1972).

3.2 "LET'S SAY *GRACE!*" (GRACE, PART ONE)

In our family growing up, "grace" referred to the prayer said before a meal. Five hungry children would exclaim "Let's say grace!" so that we could dig in. While grace may indicate a before-the-meal prayer, its meaning goes much deeper.

Beyond the before-the-meal prayer and the traditional religious definition of unmerited favour, what does grace mean? Merriam-Webster gives the following synonyms: "benevolence, mercy, blessing."[34] While these synonyms shed some light, they don't even begin to plumb the depths of this concept. As noted by Anne Lamott, "I do not understand the mystery of grace—only that it meets us where we are and does not leave us where it found us."[35] Truly, grace—from God, others, and toward ourselves—brings meaning and can change us.

Within this meditation, we look at grace to us from God. In later meditations, we speak of human grace—from ourselves to others, as well as toward ourselves. Finally, we delve into the concept of grace that is misapplied.

---

34   *Merriam-Webster Thesaurus*, s.v. "Grace," accessed May 6, 2019, https://www.merriam-webster.com/thesaurus/grace.

35   "Anne Lamott Quotes." *Goodreads.* Accessed May 6, 2019. https://www.goodreads.com/quotes/45081-i-do-not-understand-the-mystery-of-grace----only.

Experiencing grace from God can be life transforming. These blessings may come in the form of forgiven sin, healing from a terrible sickness in our own bodies or the bodies of loved ones, safety in a perilous journey ... the list goes on and on. The common denominator in these circumstances is our own powerlessness and the recognition of that helplessness to bring about what we need. When the desired result happens, we immediately think, *Oh, thank God!* And indeed, God be praised. Sometimes, however, the daily graces we receive aren't that obvious; we need to purposefully open our eyes to see how God has bestowed His grace upon us.

If we allow these mercies and blessings to seep deeply into our souls, our lives will be revolutionized. We will savour the presence of a loved one at the dinner table, be grateful for good health, rejoice in the freedom of heart to sing. We'll experience thankfulness—precisely the right response to grace. Before psychology emphasized the need for gratefulness, the scriptures stressed it. The psalmist said it well: *"Give thanks to the Lord, for he is good; his love endures forever"* (Psalm 106:1). In the messiness of our need—illness, potential tragedy, a sin-sick soul—we can find deep meaning in God's grace toward us. That grace impacts how we live our lives in relation to God, as well as in relation to humanity.

"And be thankful" (Colossians 3:15b).

3.3 "THERE BUT FOR THE GRACE OF GOD ..." (GRACE, PART TWO)

Those who have known grace—benevolence, mercy, fa-vour—from others, including God, are more likely to ex-tend it to others. The generous extension of grace from us to others, and from others to us, brings great meaning. But as the meaning is in the dirt, so the meaning is in our need for grace—and this presupposes being in touch with our own fail-ures and frailties.

Every one of us in this epic battle called life struggles with our own attitudes, behaviours, and thoughts. If we don't ever feel badly about how we behaved in a certain circumstance, are challenged by personal biases/prejudices, or get caught in thinking patterns that would leave us deeply ashamed if others knew our thoughts, then we likely lack empathy and perhaps are narcissistic. Struggle is part of the journey, so there will be times when we need to apologize to others, when we find that we have literally or metaphorically stepped on toes, behaved badly, spoken rashly, or lacked feeling.

Grace from others changes us. In situations where we re-alize that we don't deserve forgiveness, the grace of others can reach into the deep recesses of our souls. If we truly under-stand what it takes for others to extend grace toward us, we won't abuse their grace by continuing to intentionally offend or hurt them. Something within us shifts to view ourselves as flawed but known and loved. Ideally, we become more willing to extend grace toward others within our spheres. That grace may extend to people we don't even know. Being in touch with our own weaknesses, we may understand the vulnerabilities of others—the mentally ill, the addicted, the homeless. "There but for the grace of God go I."[36]

How does grace toward others add to our meaning in life? Those who truly recognize their blessings as gifts are more likely to give of themselves to the needy. Supporting worthwhile causes, whether financially or through our time, becomes more than a chore or a perceived moral responsibility. It becomes a way to express God's grace and the grace of others that we have experienced. *"Freely you have received; freely give,"* said Jesus (Matthew 10:8).

---

36   This proverb has sometimes been attributed to Christian preacher John Bradford (circa 1510–1555). However, this is in doubt by some, and has, by now, passed into common usage. For more information, see "There but for the Grace of God." *PhraseFinder*. Accessed August 22, 2019. https://www.phrases.org.uk/meanings/there-but-for-the-grace-of-god.html.

3.4 GRACE TOWARD OURSELVES (GRACE, PART THREE)

God's mercy and grace give me hope—for myself, and for our world.[37]

—Billy Graham

For some people, extending grace *toward themselves* is more difficult than believing that God offers grace, or accepting the grace of others. Even if they theoretically believe God gives grace to them, or that others forgive them, self-forgiveness somehow eludes them.[38] This may be related to a strict and rigid faith environment in their childhood, where rules were strongly emphasized, or to an upbringing in which love seemed conditional. Coming to the point where they can look at their past mistakes and forgive themselves can be transformational. This may come through aging, when their outlook on life changes. Not only do they see that others have made many of the same mistakes, but they now have *the courage to offer themselves the same grace they extend to others.* Further, if they examine the lives of people of faith (as expressed

---

37 "Billy Graham Quotes." *BrainyQuote.* Accessed May 22, 2019. https://www.brainyquote.com/quotes/billy_graham_446521?src=t_grace.

38 Annette M. Lane and Marlette B. Reed, *Older Adults: Understanding and Facilitating Transitions*, 3rd Ed. (Kendall Hunt: Dubuque, IA, 2019), 215–217.

in the Christian scriptures), they may recognize that the same One who forgave the missteps of the saints of old also forgives them, freeing them to forgive themselves.

Buddhists espouse a concept of self-compassion. While some individuals are too easy on themselves, explaining away hurtful behaviours and attitudes toward others (lacking empathy), most people err on the other side by not allowing themselves to be human—making mistakes and forgiving themselves for those errors. God's mercy extends to Billy Graham and to the world, including us. Can we extend that mercy toward ourselves?

> We all make mistakes, don't we? But if you can't forgive yourself, you'll always be an exile in your own life.[39]
>
> —Curtis Sittenfeld

---

39 "Forgive Yourself Sayings and Quotes." *wise old sayings*. Accessed August 24, 2019. http://www.wiseoldsayings.com/forgiving-your-self-quotes/.

3.5 SPACIOUS LIVES (PART ONE): FOCUSING ON THE OUTER WORLD

As mentioned earlier, I am too small for myself. Focusing on self solely results in a lack of meaning in life. An answer to self-preoccupation is to live a spacious life. How do we do that?

First, we become open to others. This means becoming genuinely interested in others' lives and listening carefully to the details of their stories, maybe even committing those details to memory. Then when we see them, even in passing, we can ask about their family members, their work, or a new project. In entering into others' lives, we can see appreciation on their faces, and that alone adds meaning to our day. But there's more. By engaging others, our world enlarges. We find ourselves thinking about the challenges and blessings in others' lives, dwelling less on ourselves and our disappointments. (Why is it so easy to focus on regrets rather than blessings?) Reflecting upon others' lives challenges us to think differently about ourselves; we may be going through difficult times, but others are experiencing equally, if not greater, trying circumstances. Our world grows larger as we ponder how others cope with unthinkable trials, and we may learn coping strategies from them. We may become more thankful for the blessings we have.

The second part of focusing on the outer world is to become open to new experiences and opportunities. Some people can't get enough of new activities and are constantly trying new things. But many of us, especially as we get older, gravitate toward the "comfortable." For the adventurous reader, you don't need encouragement to try new things! But for the one who's set in their ways, may we suggest modifying comfortable activities to include some degree of newness?

Since we're writing about living spaciously, let's use physical space as an example. Walking in one's neighbourhood is lovely, but trekking the same route every day can lead to boredom. What about an "urban hike" in another neighbourhood? Some large urban areas have books dedicated to walks throughout their districts that provide relevant facts and indicate points of interest, allowing you to plan your routes easily. By bringing a friend on the hike, you more than double the value of the experience. Not only do you see new sites, but you can dialogue with your buddy about them.

Living spaciously means focusing on others and being open to new experiences and opportunities. Are there other things that come to your mind when you think of living spaciously?

3.6 Making Connections

Connecting with others in day-to-day life is so important. In this day of fierce independence, texting, and virtual reality, face-to-face connections suffer. This is unfortunate, as making connections is one aspect of working in the dirt of meaning.

Meaningful connection sometimes occurs in a chance meeting, where we discuss concerns about one another, our communities, and the world in which we live. More than one hurting heart has been soothed by such a serendipitous encounter in a grocery store! However, trusted, sustained relationships over time are more likely to carry us through difficult life transitions, such as health challenges or the death of a loved one.

The key element here is *trust*. In the presence of trust, we can share with these safe others our fears, hopes, and vulnerabilities. The connection itself, in the dirt of life, is meaningful; however, we also may gain a sense of assurance that we will get through difficult transitions with others' care. As noted in Ecclesiastes 4:9–10: *"Two are better than one ... If either of them falls down, one can help the other up. But pity anyone who falls and has no one to pick them up."* Unfortunately, few individuals are willing to walk with us through a divorce, a family problem, a lengthy illness, or an emotional response to an acute, serious illness.

As connections with others are so important in our journey through life, it's useful to ask ourselves some questions: Who are my significant connections? How do I maintain and nurture those connections? How do I meaningfully help those I love and connect with to navigate their own challenging transitions?

Sometimes our inability to walk with others through their difficult transitions is related to our fear. The gruelling event of another disturbs us: What if this were me? So we withdraw. But, remembering that empathy is essential, we should ask ourselves, "What if this were me?" and extend ourselves.

Don't wait until a crisis to make meaningful connections; rather, make the time to develop those relationships in your everyday life. When a person who's important to us (a significant connection) faces a crisis, we'll know the best way to respond because of our knowledge of them. Also, when we encounter troubles, our "call at three o'clock in the morning" relationships are in place.

Friends love through all kinds of weather, and families stick together in all kinds of trouble.

—Proverbs 17:17 (MSG)

3.7 Choosing Our Trusted Others Carefully

Love all, trust a few, do wrong to none.[40]

—William Shakespeare

In the previous meditation, we addressed the importance of making connections. Connections bring meaning to our day-to-day living and can be invaluable when we experience difficulties. However, our choices regarding who we trust are important, as not everyone is worthy of our trust.

As young people, we may feel pride over the number of friends we have. Our friend count on social media may elevate (or lower) our self-worth. As we age, however, we realize that it's hard to sustain many friendships, and that quality may be more critical than quantity. We may also recognize that while some friends may be fun to be around, they may not necessarily understand us, or be careful of our feelings when we let down our guard and share our challenges.

How do we form trusting relationships to sustain us through difficult times? A good place to start is to look for friends that share our set of values. Do these people value what we value—living lives that make a difference in this world? We may also keep our eyes open for how they deal with the

---

40 "Trust Quotes." *Goodreads*. Accessed August 19, 2019. https://www.goodreads.com/quotes/tag/trust.

misfortunes of others. Do they feel badly for others who are experiencing difficult times and try to help them? If they don't care for the feelings of others, they likely won't care for ours.

We can kibitz with friends, but do they seem concerned when we share that a loved one is experiencing health problems, or has lost a job? Such problems are connected to us but not necessarily too personal. If they do seem concerned, they may be careful (full of care) when we share something that impacts us greatly. Further, do these friends keep confidences, or do they freely share others' confidences with us? Those who do not keep others' confidences are unlikely to keep ours.

While we can never fully predict how friends may respond when we experience a crisis, the above considerations may help us in our discernment. While King David knew countless people, he had to be very careful in whom he trusted—dangerous is the life of a king! In I Samuel, we're told that Jonathan, perhaps David's closest friend, was "*one in spirit*" with David, and that he "*loved* [David] *as himself*" (18:1). This friendship involved shared values, fellowship, empathy, and trust. So deep was this brotherhood that Jonathan took great risks to preserve David's life. Truly, trusted friends are a gift from God.

3.8 UNDERSTANDING AND BEING UNDERSTOOD: GOING DEEP IN RELATIONSHIPS

Friendship is born at that moment when one (person) says to another: "What! You too? I thought I was the only one …"[41]

—C.S. Lewis

Our greatest needs also are our greatest vulnerabilities, so it follows that with these needs/vulnerabilities, we may face great challenges in this broken world. On the top of this list of needs is genuine relationship. It seems to be a cry of the human heart to be understood. When we don't feel understood, we experience a penetrating sense of loneliness, and such loneliness can lead to despair. Often this despair is felt most keenly at a time of adversity, when family and friends may not understand or tolerate our challenges. There's profound meaning in offering understanding to others and in being understood. For two persons in need of relationship, understanding can birth friendship. Other times, it can be a lifesaver for the person who is deeply despairing.

Offering understanding means that we listen actively and that we listen far more than we speak. Sometimes it

41 "C.S. Lewis Quotes." *Goodreads*. Accessed: August 11, 2019. https://www.goodreads.com/quotes/10554-friendship-is-born-at-the-moment-when-one-man.

means not speaking at all. Job's comforters did their finest work when they sat silently with the stricken Job for seven days and nights (Job 2:13).[42] Parker Palmer claims that this type of understanding—being truly present but without platitudes or explanations—is to stand "respectfully at the edge of that person's mystery and misery."[43] It requires a knowledge of the frailty of humanity—that we are all closer to adversity than we'd like to admit—and is very rare. It doesn't require understanding of every human problem; rather, it necessitates an understanding of what it is to suffer. Is there someone in your life who's been able to provide this type of care for you? Did you find being understood at this level helpful?

At times input may be welcome, but only when the hurting person *knows* they're understood. With understanding, concern, and humility, we can then listen and discuss (if this is what they want) the situation. There may come a time when we can point the individual to appropriate help. There's no timetable for getting through deep adversity, so there's no timetable for understanding. Certainly we must set boundaries, as we cannot help everyone indefinitely. But we were meant to live with this type of presence—understanding and (hopefully) being understood.

A friend loves at all times, and a brother is born for a time of adversity.

—Proverbs 17:17

---

42 Ironically, now the term "Job's comforters" is an epithet for those who are particularly poor in understanding others. Job's friends would have been remembered differently had they stayed silent, rather than, after the seven days and nights, deluged Job with their poor explanations.

43 Parker J. Palmer, *Let Your Life Speak* (San Francisco, CA: Jossey-Bass, 2000), 63.

3.9 LEARNING ACROSS THE LIFESPAN

Anyone who stops learning is old, whether at twenty
or eighty. Anyone who keeps learning stays young.[44]
—Henry Ford

There is tremendous meaning in learning, no matter our age! While children *must* go to school, learning is often a choice when we become adults. For some, the learning will take place in an area that interests them creatively, such as flower arranging or cooking ethnic foods. Others will pursue certifications in their recreational interests, such as SCUBA diving or flying planes. Still others will pursue mastery for mastery's sake and perhaps learn a new language.

This curiosity about life is a wonderful thing! We knew an individual many years ago who stated that she had accomplished all her life goals by the age of twenty. As we reflected upon this, we sincerely hoped that her aims in life—curiosity, goals to achieve, things to learn—grew as she aged. Otherwise, using Ford's idea, this precious lady would have been very old at a very young age.

The benefits of life-long learning are well-known. Not only do individuals engage their brains in understanding new

---

44 "Lifelong Learning Quotes." *Goodreads.* Accessed June 9, 2019. https://
www.goodreads.com/quotes/tag/lifelong-learning.

ideas or making connections between ideas, but the learning adds structure to their days. Going to class means that part of a day or evening is spent travelling to and from an institution. Individuals meet others and may strategize on how to help each other. Those who study online may attend webinars, and although this may not be face-to-face interaction, they still will engage with others, as well as with ideas.

What is learned—irrespective of the educational venue—can become a source of meaningful conversation between learners and their children, siblings, and friends. The return to learning is also a wonderful example to others, particularly younger generations. Students who return to school in adulthood exemplify a love of learning, a willingness to take risks—for instance, a seventy-year old who returns to university to pursue a master's degree—and the importance of filling life with meaningful activities.

We have co-taught a master's level course at a university where every student but one was in their late fifties to mid-sixties. All but one were embarking on a new paid or volunteer career in ministry. Their enthusiasm, humour, intelligence, and ability to process and interact with ideas were inspiring. And they were truly youthful!

The education of a man is never completed until he dies.[45]

—Robert E. Lee

45 "Time Quotes." *BrainyQuote.* Accessed June 4, 2019. https://www.brainyquote.com/quotes/earl_nightingale_159030?src=t_time.

3.10 Work and Meaning

We are at our very best, and we are happiest, when
we are fully engaged in work we enjoy on the journey
toward the goal we we've established for ourselves.
It gives meaning to our time off and comfort to our
sleep. It makes everything else in life so wonderful,
so worthwhile.[46]

—Earl Nightingale

Sometimes work gets a bad rap! We all know people who,
when asked how their work is going, reply, "Well, you
know, work is work." They don't say this with enthusiasm but
with apathy and perhaps a palpable tone of drudgery. These
individuals may believe that work is only useful insofar as it
allows them to pay their bills, but nothing more.

As noted by Nightingale, when we're truly engaged in our
work (challenged in a positive sense), and our work aligns with
our goals in life, we can be truly happy. Our work also needs to
line up with our personality characteristics and life paradigm,
our core values. For example, a very sensitive person may value the law but may not be well-suited for police work over the
long term. We know of a minister who valued helping people;

---

46   "Time Quotes." *BrainyQuote.* Accessed June 4, 2019. https://www.brainy-
quote.com/quotes/earl_nightingale_159030?src=t_time.

however, the constraints of his job required that he preach each week. This didn't align with his natural shyness, and he vomited before each sermon. He didn't remain in this position for long.[47]

Regarding core values, caring individuals may enter health care professions, while social workers, valuing social justice, may work with vulnerable populations such as the homeless or troubled adolescents. Those who believe in the power of education to shape and change lives may enter teaching. Despite the challenges of working with people, particularly those in difficult circumstances, as well as larger system problems and constraints, the deep satisfaction of expressing our personhood through our work, in alignment with our personalities and values, can be extremely meaningful. And, as Nightingale indicated, the meaning in our work can infuse our days off with meaning, as the satisfaction emanating from our work nourishes us even when we aren't working.

> If you do what you love, you'll never work a day in your life.[48]
>
> —Marc Anthony

---

47   There are many ministers for whom preaching is a problem; they can work very effectively within large, multi-staff churches, doing what they are suited for.

48   "Do What You Love Quotes." *BrainyQuote*. Accessed August 7, 2019. https://www.brainyquote.com/topics/do_what_you_love.

3.11 REASONABLE RISKS REQUIRED

We're all risk averse creatures, aren't we? Like tur-
tles, hiding in our little shells, trying to protect ourselves—never quite realising that we're protecting
ourselves from the good stuff as well as the bad.[49]

—Debbie Johnson

Not all readers will agree with Johnson. Indeed, North
Americans engage in a plethora of pursuits today precisely
to take risks! Some people die doing extreme sports—risk-tak-
ing that wasn't necessary. We are not advocating this. However, we are saying that in order to have a meaningful life, some
reasonable risk (to use my husband, Brian's, term) is necessary.
Many people in this age of perfectionism don't take reasonable
risks for fear of failure. (Are you aware of the term "snowplow
parenting"? It refers to well-meaning parents who remove all
obstacles from their children growing up so that these kids don't
experience failure.[50]) Without learning to face obstacles through

49 "Risk Taking Quotes." *Goodreads*. Accessed August 24, 2019. https://
www.goodreads.com/quotes/tag/risk-taking?page=2.

50 See Michael Alcee, "What Snowplow Parenting Misses: The Benefits of
Creative Struggle," *Psychology Today*, June 12, 2019. Accessed: August
24, 2019, https://www.psychologytoday.com/us/blog/live-life-creative-
ly/201906/what-snowplow-parenting-misses.

reasonable risk, kids and adults don't learn how to tolerate anxiety and experience failure. We play life so safe, we don't grow. As mentioned in the introduction, people who want a risk-free life ("sanitized") may struggle with meaning at some point. While "safe" (not risking failure or criticism), these lives are often dull. Psychologist Michael Alcee speaks about snowplow parenting, stating that some struggle is necessary for children as well as adults. We all need this to truly know ourselves. "We become more ourselves and more a part of this wildly unpredictable yet heartbreakingly beautiful world. That, in the end, is worth the struggle."[51] In knowing what we can and *cannot do,* we understand ourselves much better than if we had hidden in our turtle shells.

Through reasonable risk taking, we understand our calling better, and here the stakes are higher. Remember the sobering parable of the talents in Matthew 25:14–30? Three servants were given a portion of their master's money (*talents* in the KJV) to manage while he was away. The first two servants doubled the investment; the third, wanting to play it safe, buried it. Rather than receiving an "I understand" from the master when he returned, this third individual was severely reprimanded. *"It's criminal to live cautiously like that! If you knew I was after the best, why did you do less than the least?"* (Matthew 25:26–27, MSG).

Our calling and our abilities (talents) are given to us not simply to bless *us,* but also to bless *others.* Reasonable risk taking is necessary to knowing ourselves, developing our talents, and investing them in others. Failure to do this robs us of a meaningful life, but it also deprives others and buries our Master's investment.

---

51   Ibid.

3.12 Seeing Meaning in Everyday Life

The stuff of everyday life —the common turf of living—often seems boring and mundane. Within Western societies, the extraordinary is praised, as some want thrills, chills, and spills! Surely the chores and regular activities of daily life cannot be that important or meaningful, can they?

In a previous book, we addressed meaning in the "mundane."[52] We wrote of the importance of normal, everyday life in the lives of aging adults; however, normalcy can take on extra significance for everyone, regardless of age, when our lives are turned upside down. When lives are hijacked by uncontrollable, difficult circumstances (e.g., illness, unemployment, or caring for an ill relative), the usual activities of daily living take on added importance. The ability to perform regular chores in the household affirms personhood, of which control and mastery are components. For instance, those with early-onset dementia (dementia prior to age sixty-five) want to hold on to family roles for as long as they can, thus demonstrating that they are still vital.[53]

---

52   Lane and Reed, *Making Meaning.*

53   M.L. Sakamoto, S.L. Moore, and S.T. Johnson, "'I'm still here': Personhood and the Early-Onset Dementia Experience," *Journal of Gerontological Nursing* 43, no. 5 (2017): 12–17.

Everyday activities and routine also give us structure, perpetuating a sense of normalcy—tasks that were once annoying now become comforting. If we're unable to complete the mundane activities of life, we may find that we long for when we could, as they represented control and a regular life. Also, relationships that are taken for granted may now become more precious. They remind us that although life is difficult and has changed—perhaps never to return to what it once was—life still has some normal aspects and we can gain "a new normal"[54] in the future.

> It's the simple things in your life that make up the bulk of it. The mundane is where we live, and we end up missing most of it. We find it again in the silence and in attention of everyday life.[55]
>
> —Eric Overby

---

54 This term is often used in grief literature. A person who has lost a loved one will not "get over it." But, over time, and having worked through their grief, they may achieve a "new normal." This seems fitting here, as when the unexpected has changed life, there is grief and then a "new normal" must often be achieved.

55 "Everyday Life Quotes." *Goodreads*. Accessed July 25, 2019. https://www.goodreads.com/quotes/tag/everyday-life.

3.13 RICHNESS IN MORTALITY: TIME AND PERCEPTION

Every day is a gift and a very special day; so, let us celebrate with joy and profound gratitude.[56]

—Debasish Mridha

This life is for loving, sharing, learning, smiling, caring ...[57]

—Steve Maraboli

When we're young, life seems to stretch on forever. We long for holidays, and when they come, we can easily become bored. We may also long for adulthood, believing that the freedoms it affords will provide more fun. Days may be wasted with no thought, knowing we have many, many decades ahead of us.

When we become adults, we realize that with freedom comes responsibility and that we didn't appreciate the unfettered joys of our childhood. The current pressures of work and the cares of providing for ourselves and/or our families can invite us to long for the past or the distant future—retirement.

---

56 "Every Day is a Gift Quotes." *Goodreads.* Accessed July 11, 2019. https://www.goodreads.com/quotes/tag/everyday-is-a-gift.

57 "Sharing Quotes." *Goodreads.* Accessed July 11, 2019. https://www.goodreads.com/quotes/tag/sharing.

As we did in our youth, we may waste time wishing that we were in a different life stage or situation.

Mridha invites us to live in the present, viewing each day with appreciation rather than dread or boredom. Maraboli's words encourage us to share our time and *ourselves* with others in a meaningful way. Why is it that so often we don't realize these things until there's an untimely death in our family, or we become seriously ill or enter old age? Once we appreciate the brevity of life, we may begin to cherish our days, as well as our family and friends. The common things—laughter with a friend, a thick, creamy chocolate milkshake, the singing birds in the trees—become rich experiences. While our newfound discovery helps us make the most of our remaining days, we may regret not having arrived at this epiphany sooner. Our challenge is to embrace life daily before crises remind us of its transience. The dirt of our mortality, when recognized and embraced, adds substance to our lives. Moses recognized this, and in an impassioned plea to God cried out, *"Oh! Teach us to live well! Teach us to live wisely and well!"* (Psalm 90:12, MSG).

3.14 Encouragement: Bringing Courage to Another

Within popular culture, the word "encouragement" is often used to denote praise or compliments, or it screams "Way to go!" from the sidelines of a soccer field. While this is part of encouragement, more is involved. According to one source, the origin of the word "encourage" is to make, or put in, courage.[58] Jenn Arman, speaking about the 105 times the Greek word for encouragement (parakaleo) is used in the New Testament, indicates that it's used to develop something in the one being encouraged; the encourager teaches, comforts, strengthens, and even pushes the one they're encouraging.[59] While we're cautious about pushing people, these verbs definitely strengthen the meaning of encouragement.

To impart courage to someone, to seek to develop something in another, is an incredible privilege and meaningful to the encourager as well as to the individual receiving encouragement. Encouragement should be specific to the person as well as to his or her situation or personality. It also should be sincere and without ulterior motives, as most people can detect

---

58 *Online Etymology Dictionary*, s.v. "Encourage," accessed May 5, 2019, https://www.etymonline.com/word/encourage.

59 Jenn Arman, "What Does Encouragement Really Mean?" *Project Inspired*, accessed August 8, 2019. https://www.projectinspired.com/bible-study-what-does-encouragement-really-mean/.

insincerity. When we as encouragers sense that we're giving support because we want to get something from the person, the nourishing waters of our motivation have become brackish. To encourage someone in a specific and honest manner, the encourager needs to observe an individual, listen carefully to what they say, and then choose an appropriate time to offer feedback. Encouraging others comes naturally for some, but for others it's more difficult.

The impact of encouragement can be profound. Many successful individuals credit the powerful influence of a teacher or mentor. They describe how an individual saw strengths and abilities in them that no one else did, including themselves. The encouragement of this important person helped them see themselves differently, and hence pursue interests and careers. The results were life changing!

> Too often we underestimate the power of a touch, a smile, a kind word, a listening ear, an honest compliment, or the smallest act of caring, all of which have the potential to turn a life around.[60]
>
> —Leo Buscaglia

> *Gently encourage the stragglers, and reach out for the exhausted, pulling them to their feet. Be patient with each person, attentive to individual needs. And be careful that when you get on each other's nerves you don't snap at each other. Look for the best in each other, and always do your best to bring it out.*
>
> —1 Thessalonians 5:14–15 (MSG)

---

60 "Leo Buscaglia Quotes." *BrainyQuote.* Accessed May 5, 2019. https://www.brainyquote.com/authors/leo-buscaglia-quotes.

3.15 FINDING BEAUTY IN LOVELY AND UNLOVELY CIRCUMSTANCES

As we have written elsewhere, meaning can be found in recognizing and enjoying beauty.[61] This makes sense, as most of us have experienced times when we've driven into the mountains and felt that the beauty and grandeur of the rock has almost sucked the breath out of us. Walking in a mixed forest in the fall, with the dark-green pine needles interspersed with the brilliant yellow and orange deciduous leaves, infuses us with a sense of awe and peace. The rich smell of the fallen leaves decaying in the soil reminds us of the life cycle—those leaves so new in spring go to the ground and, in death, nourish the earth. Many of us find that the beauty of nature confirms our belief in the creative power of God.

It's helpful to remember a couple of important points about beauty. First, we can become so immersed in our lives and problems that we don't see the beauty. We may physically see the glorious colours of fall yet fail to see and experience that beauty in our hearts. The ability to be present *in* the moment, *to the beauty of the moment*, is lost, and so is the opportunity to nourish our souls.

Second, we can look for beauty in places that aren't naturally seen as beautiful. As noted by Salma Hayek:

---

61   Lane and Reed, *Making Meaning in Older Age*, 52–54.

People say that 'beauty is in the eye of the beholder,' but I say that the most liberating thing about beauty is realizing that you are the beholder. This empowers us to find beauty in places where others have not dared to look, including inside ourselves.[62]

If we as beholders of beauty choose to look for beauty in dark circumstances, we may be surprised to find our souls nourished in those difficult situations. This requires effort and discipline. Finding beauty in crises, such as a natural disaster, the illness or death of a loved one, or the loss of a job, may involve seeing the kindness of others, the courage of our loved ones, and/or in the joy of reconnecting with former friends and the formation of new relationships. Finding beauty in difficult places was one of the many surprises for me when I started to work with dying people. In death, life's meanings were affirmed; in death, life was nourished. "I'll never be the same again!" was expressed to me repeatedly by people who found beauty in the community of hospice, in the challenges and growth of journeying with a dying family member, of finding God present in the midst of life and death.

62 "Beauty Quotes." *Goodreads*. Accessed July 4, 2019. https://www.goodreads.com/quotes/109192-people-often-say-that-beauty-is-in-the-eye-of.

3.16 LISTENING: AN UNCOMMON SKILL

Good listeners are hard to find in this world of extreme noise, busyness, and rush. It seems that very few people are adept at the skill of truly listening. Listening requires a degree of quiet; it also takes time. Many of us have few quiet spaces or moments to spend with others. Also, some may feel that listening is too passive, or that it prevents them from sharing about themselves. But true listening is incredibly active. It's an expression of our personhood that reveals that we're comfortable being with ourselves (without validating ourselves to others) and with others (in their joy, pain, or even dreariness). How is this so?

As a wise sage once said, "To listen carefully ... this can be our greatest gift to one we love." Listening is a precious gift to others. It involves conscientious attention to the words of the speaker as well as his or her tone of voice and non-verbal behaviour. A careful listener will show by his or her attention that what the speaker says, and even does not say, is meaningful and important. When the listener does speak, words are chosen thoughtfully and in a way that doesn't derail the speaker's need to process a difficult situation.

After much listening, with carefully placed words or questions to clarify, a listener then has earned the right to offer insights, support, and suggestions. However, the input should be given with grace, respect, and an understanding of *timing*.

Job's comforters certainly provided Job with much bad insight and advice, but at least they had the sense before they spoke to sit silently with Job for seven days and seven nights (Job 2:13). It would have been better to offer the gift of listening rather than foisting upon their hurting friend the "present" of unwanted advice!

3.17 Looking for Love and Mercy in All the Right Places

The Lord's unfailing love and mercy still continue, fresh as the morning, as sure as the sunrise.
—Lamentations 3:22–23 (GNT)

What we focus upon in our daily lives partly determines what we see. If we look for the negative, we will surely find it! We'll find appalling situations in the media, and we'll find ourselves riveted to the troubling and difficult circumstances in our own lives or the lives of others. Some of us work in professions where we see ugliness and tragedy regularly. Obviously, we can't totally escape tribulation within this world, and we don't want to shy away from others who are experiencing challenging or grim situations.

If we can't turn away from the discouraging events in the world, our work, or our families, how can we respond in productive and healthy ways? The verse from Lamentations provides a constructive response. In the angst of life, we need to remind ourselves that God's *"unfailing love and mercy still continue."* This positions us to look for that love and mercy daily. What situations that we witness or experience show God's love and compassion? In what ways? How do these encouraging events trigger us to show love and mercy to others?

I look for examples of love and beauty wherever I go. When a church service seems to be going longer than the comfort level of my joints, I focus on a parent tousling his toddler's hair, or the obvious love for God on an elderly woman's face as she sings. In these examples, I see God's love and mercy around me: The Creator of love and life reveals Himself in people. This *unfailing love and mercy* can also be seen in the buds on the trees in spring and the sun that rises each morning. Examples of this can bring a smile to my face, which is then given to those around me—and the grace of God continues.

Vital to this discipline, the ability to focus on God's love and mercy is predicated upon limiting the negativity in our lives. If we expose ourselves to too much ugliness, specifically that which is *voluntary* (such as disturbing movies or television shows), we can easily lose our focus. In this regard, meaning is *not* in the dirt.

It seems odd that we need encouragement to regularly consider the Lord's love and mercy; however, we often don't realize that we're bombarded by destructive messages regularly. Could a daily practice of looking for God's love and mercy become a spiritual discipline in our lives? What a difference this could make!

3.18 Practicing Intelligent Compassion: Exercising Heart and Mind

The true measure of any society can be found in how it treats its weakest members.[63]

—Mahatma Gandhi

Few would argue with the need for compassion for those who are suffering or vulnerable, such as children, aging adults, those with developmental disabilities, and animals. Compassion is integral to the strength of a society, including its moral fibre. Helping others in difficult circumstances, as well as receiving help when needed, brings meaning to our lives. There is meaning in the dirt!

Compassion needs to be woven together with intelligence and discernment, however. As we were growing up, our dad would say: "Helping people is the most difficult task of all." As teenagers, we didn't understand this; we thought that helping others was quite straightforward. Give individuals what they need. (Honestly, we believed that!)

We hadn't considered the need to balance helping others with their need to take responsibility for themselves. Helpers, in helping too much (sometimes out of the need to be needed), may unwittingly strip others of their dignity by taking away

---

63 "Mahatma Gandhi Quotes." *AZ Quotes*. Accessed June 23, 2019. https://www.azquotes.com/author/5308-Mahatma_Gandhi.

their agency, responsibility, and power. In the immediate, helpers may feel a great sense of satisfaction and have the need for significance met. But repeatedly rushing in to help individuals may teach them that they *do not have to* and that they *do not have the wherewithal to* address the issues that led to their problems. Despite their best intentions, helpers may hurt others, even while trying to "help" them.

It has become clear in our years of working with others that we need to bring together our hearts (compassion) and our intelligence (discernment) to truly help others. As the common proverb says, "Give a man a fish and you feed him for a day; show him how to catch fish and you feed him for a lifetime."[64] Weaving together heart and mind in helping actions assures both help and health for the individual in need.

---

64 This quotation is attributed to a number of sources. BrainyQuote credits medieval Jewish philosopher Maimonides with this proverb. See "Maimonides Quotes." *BrainyQuote.* Accessed July 25, 2019. https://www.brainyquote.com/quotes/maimonides_326751.

3.19 THE FUNCTIONALITY OF FUN

Meaning-making isn't always enjoyable; much effort can be expended in slogging through the dirt while planting our garden. This dirt can come in the form of long-term commitments, the learning of new skills, or dealing with difficult people or situations. While fun may crop up during activities that foster making meaning, these activities often aren't fun in and of themselves.

For some, having fun comes naturally within relationships or through activities (play) and hobbies. For those of us weighted down by work, caring for others, and carrying other burdens, enjoyment may seem unrealistic, unrepresentative of life, or even irresponsible. We may have lost one aspect of the "work" in childhood—to have fun through play. Eeyore's statement, "The sky has finally fallen. Always knew it would,"[65] may come all-too-easily.

Having fun is important alongside the seriousness of making meaning. The value of fun may be greater for people who are naturally serious-minded, or who carry the burdens of others deeply. Recreation (note the word: re-creation) through activities such as sports, games, travel, and sharing

---

65 "The Definitive List of Eeyore Quotes." *Oh My Disney*. Accessed July 14, 2019. https://ohmy.disney.com/quotes/2018/05/12/definitive-list-eeyore-quotes/.

coffee and conversation at a favourite diner provides *balance* to the demands of commitment while making meaning. It reminds us that while life may be solemn and grim at times, good moments are never far away. It helps us to look forward to the future, or at least parts of the future, where we can burn off steam in a game of racquetball, laugh, or enjoy a great meal with people we care about. It also provides structure so that we're not tempted to work during non-working hours, or to excessively stew about problems within our lives.

Ironically, we may need to purposefully schedule fun events in our lives to ensure that we actually take time for enjoyment. When we afford ourselves time for fun, we may find that we're more effective in the activities that foster making meaning. Why? Because we have re-created!

> It is more fun to talk with someone who doesn't use long, difficult words but rather short, easy words like, "What about lunch?"[66]
>
> —Winnie the Pooh

---

66 "Winnie the Pooh Quotes." *Overall Motivation.* Accessed July 14, 2019. https://www.overallmotivation.com/quotes/best-winnie-the-pooh-quotes-life/.

3.20 GRATITUDE: MENTAL TOUGHNESS IN ACTION

When we were growing up, our father used to talk about the importance of having "an attitude of gratitude." Dad's emphasis on this was partly related to his Christian faith, but it was also shaped by his time spent in a forced labour camp during World War II. He and our mother knew what it was like to experience hunger, uncertainty, and fear during World War II in occupied Holland.

As daughters, we *were* grateful for what we received. We regularly thanked our parents and were respectful to teachers and those in authority. However, we probably failed to understand the deeper meaning of Dad's words—regularly and consistently expressing gratitude to God, whether we liked our circumstances or not.

As adults having experienced a number of life's challenges, the discipline of having "an attitude of gratitude" takes on greater meaning. It requires a mental toughness to consistently recognize God's hand in our lives, both when things are (relatively) easy and when our circumstances skid sideways. Perhaps this is why the Apostle Paul said, *"give thanks in all circumstances; for this is God's will for you in Christ Jesus"* (1 Thessalonians 5:18). In this passage of scripture, Paul doesn't instruct us to give thanks *for* all things but *in* every circumstance. As we've been working on this book, Annette has been battling Stage Four cancer. After one of her surgeries, she stayed at the Reed House for a few days of recuperation. She and I watched playoff sports and quiz shows on TV; when she needed to move her temporarily disabled leg, I would help her reposition. When she needed help getting up, this was provided. While neither of us expressed gratitude for the cancer, we spoke of the blessing of hanging out together—we hadn't spent so much time together since we were children! What a blessing this was to me!

We are human and often struggle to see God's hand in very difficult situations. This is, in part, why we're instructed to show mental toughness through giving thanks *in* everything. By that act of trust, our eyes may be opened to see blessings and goodness in the midst of difficulty. It's always godly to ask for grace to respond constructively (rather than bitterly) to challenges and to thank Him that He works out our circumstances for good (Romans 8:28), even if we can't see it.

3.21 Developing Empathy in Adulthood

In Section Two, we highlighted the character quality of *empathy* as essential for deep relationships and meaning in life. As you were reading, you may have been hit with a pang or two of regret or even anger: "What about those of us who didn't get this type of modelling and teaching in our formative years?" While this is unfortunate and has surely affected you up to this point, there are always opportunities to learn empathy.

Think back on people's comments toward you. Have people ever told you that your responses are harsh? This may reveal a shortage of empathy in you. On September 11, 2001, when staff in the company where my husband worked became aware of the attacks on the World Trade Center and the Pentagon, a number of people wept. One man said, "Not my problem!" This individual lacked the ability to put himself in another's shoes.

You may also wish to do a "temperature check" with a couple of trusted persons in your life. Ask them: "Do you experience empathy from me? When you're struggling, do you feel I show understanding?" Their responses may reveal an opportunity for growth in your life.

Pray about your perspectives on life. The Holy Spirit is called the *"Counselor"* (John 14:26, MEV); in other translations, He's called the *"Helper"* (NLV), the *"Friend"* (MSG), the *"Comforter"* (KJV). These are all descriptive terms of empathy. He is also the One who has been sent to *"teach you all things"*

(14:26). The ability to feel for and with others is in the will of God; you can trust Him to work at developing this within you!

Seek professional help. A skilled and empathic counsellor, coach, or pastor can be of great help to the individual who genuinely wants to grow in this area. You will know if you're this type of person by how you respond to such a professional when they give you feedback that hurts. A response of "That's it, I'm out of here!" indicates that you may not be ready to do this type of personality work. Tears and trust in this individual's urging to revise your perspectives and responses are indicative of your desire and readiness to truly grow.

From here, begin to give of yourself in ways that will stretch you *a bit*. We don't recommend diving into the deep end of volunteering with incarcerated individuals (for the sake of the vulnerable others and for yourself).[67] But perhaps you can bless others by ushering in church. As it takes time for empathy to develop in a child, so it does in adulthood. Take small steps.

Can you give yourself and others the gift of empathy?

---

67 Employees and volunteers must always be vetted through the proper channels; the safety of others is paramount.

3.22 LEARNING TO HOLD SPACE

Have you ever known someone who could sit with you in your pain without trying to fix it? This person wasn't prescriptive in how you should handle your difficulties; rather, they thoughtfully and carefully sat with you. They held space for you; it was a precious gift of presence.

According to Heather Plett, a person who holds space doesn't take the hurting person's power away; his/her own intuition and wisdom is validated. If I'm holding space, I must keep my own ego out of the interaction. (It's not what *I* think the person needs but what that person feels that he/she needs that's important.) This means allowing the hurting person to make decisions that I wouldn't make myself, even if I know this course of action will fail. (So hard to do when I want to spare pain.) And, if asked, I give guidance with humility and empathy. Finally, Plett gives the wonderful metaphor of creating a container for complex emotions such as fear and guilt. In essence, I am the container that can hold another's emotions without judgement, without quick solutions, without being overcome by the emotion myself.[68]

This is a tall order! One who can do this learns the techniques of holding space. Equally important, this person has

---

68   Heather Plett, "What it Means to Hold Space for Someone." *Uplift.* May 8, 2016, https://upliftconnect.com/hold-space/.

developed in his or her own life a depth of feeling—a well, a reservoir—of human experience, as well as the knowledge and humility that goes with it. If I have occasionally "fallen apart" during difficult times, I'm much more likely to be humble and gracious with someone else who feels like they're crumbling. And I know that this won't last; this is a part of the fatigue and grief that come with larger-than-life circumstances.

As a new palliative care chaplain, I found it difficult to sit with people who were experiencing overwhelming grief. One of the most helpful things for me was finding out that the grief process works. I discovered this when these previously grief-stricken people would come back to the hospice months later and tell me that they were doing much better. This gave me the confidence within myself to hold space for those who were losing loved ones, because I *knew* they would come through.

Perhaps speaking from the perspective of one who needed space held for her, Emily Dickinson said, "I felt it shelter to speak with you."[69]

---

69 "Emily Dickinson Quotes." *Goodreads.* Accessed May 29, 2019. https://www.goodreads.com/quotes/96385-i-felt-it-shelter-to-speak-to-you.

3.23 Meaning in Aging: Opportunity and Gift for Younger Adults

In our youth-oriented society, how should younger adults respond to the aging process of others, as well as their own aging? To avoid thinking about it, only to a have crisis in mid-life, or making poor decisions to prove youthfulness, isn't helpful (and let's face it—sometimes it's downright destructive and embarrassing).

May we suggest another approach? Noted by renowned priest and author, Henry Nouwen (and co-author Walter Gaffney), younger individuals need to allow aging adults "a chance to bring (younger adults) into a creative contact with (their) own aging."[70] What an intriguing concept! The authors explain that creative contact involves aging adults teaching younger individuals about how to age with humour, purpose, and meaning. They also teach younger individuals that aging isn't to be feared; although challenges arise in aging, lives may be imbued with meaning and purpose, and this meaning may transcend their circumstances.

This contact can also be extended from younger people to older ones. I was in a nursing home recently, and while meeting with a staff member, I heard grunts of effort, squeals of delight, and shouts of triumph! The noise was so loud that our

---

70   Henri Nouwen and Walter Gaffney, *Aging: The Fulfillment of Life* (New York, NY: DoubleDay, 1974), 154.

meeting was shortened and we stood outside this staff member's office to watch the source of this unmitigated ruckus and joy. What was happening? Elementary school children were playing a modified hockey game with nursing home residents in wheelchairs. It was clear that the kids were having a ball, as were their elders. While Nouwen and Gaffney may not have had this in mind, this is truly "creative contact" between the generations; not only do older people enjoy younger people, but younger people enjoy the presence of their elders, gaining the benefits of interesting and interested older adults who are fun and who delight in them.

Although Solomon wasn't likely thinking of creative contact between generations, his words are apt: "... *those who refresh others will themselves be refreshed*" (Proverbs 11:25, NLT). Younger people and adults can learn much from their elders, including how to age well.

3.24 MEANING IN MOVEMENT DURING OLDER AGE

Research shows that living well in older age hinges strongly upon being able to keep moving.[71] Those who are mobile:

a) stay in their own homes much longer;
b) get out and about for socializing;
c) release some of those wonderful feel-good endorphins with exercise;
d) maintain their mental sharpness longer;
e) stave off the loss of muscle mass and prevent bone weakening.

I was speaking with an elderly gentleman some months ago and asked him if he was still going to the gym each weekday morning. "I have to," he replied. "It's the only way to keep going!" This gentleman volunteers in a number of different capacities, adding deeply to his well of meaning. He golfs in the

---

71 L.J. Graham and D.M. Connelly, "'Any Movement at all Is Exercise': A Focused Ethnography of Rural Community Dwelling Older Adults' Perceptions of and Experiences of Exercise as Self-Care." *Physiotherapy Canada* 65, no. 4 (2013): 333–341. doi:10.3138/ptc.2012–31, and Neil E. Peterson, Kay D. Osterloh, and M. Nichole Graff, "Exercises for Older Adults with Knee and Hip Pain." *The Journal for Nurse Practitioners* 15 (2019): 263–267.

summer in Canada and goes to sunny climes for winter recreation. And he exercises daily. A wonderful example!

Some aging adults go to exercise classes such as Tai Chi or dancing. Others incorporate movement into their daily lives without going to the gym or exercise class. They walk to the library or garden, or perhaps play golf. A key motivator tends to be exercising with one or more individuals to enhance togetherness. Some more sedate adults (not necessarily senior adults) intentionally get a dog that they'll need to walk. If they don't feel like exercising, Fido will come begging for his walk! The payoff for an owner is both pleasing the pet (who will respond to the walk with joy and affection) and feeling good about their own exercise. They may have a conversation or two along the way, adding to their meaning.

A middle-aged adult in a sedentary job recently saw his doctor for back pain. Rather than pain medication (which, it should be noted, is sometimes warranted), the physician recommended that this gentleman first get a dog that would need regular walking. In speaking with me, this individual expressed excitement about the possibility. Another motivator to keep moving is enjoyment; when activities are enjoyable, older adults may be more likely to stick with them over the long run.

When the body is aging, it's tempting to sit in a comfortable chair and participate in activities that require little physical movement. But by keeping active throughout the lifespan, people enjoy living more. "We do not stop exercising because we grow old—we grow old because we stop exercising," said Kenneth Cooper.[72]

72 "Exercise Sayings and Quotes." *wise old sayings*. Accessed August 8, 2019. http://www.wiseoldsayings.com/exercise-quotes/.

3.25 How We Respond to Those Who Are Vulnerable

How far you go in life depends on your being tender with the young, compassionate with the aged, sympathetic with the striving, and tolerant of the weak and strong. Because someday in life you will have been all of these.[73]

—George Washington Carver

Strength and productivity are lauded in our society. Weakness and vulnerability are not. Vulnerability that comes with age, ill health, or difficult situations is feared, and may, at best, be pitied. At worst, some have contempt for the weak; this may come out of their own fear of becoming weak and their worry about how they would be treated.

According to George Washington Carver, we all will experience vulnerability related to age or weakness, even if at many points in life we were strong. This knowledge should propel us to think about how we would want to be treated if we experienced great vulnerability related to paralysis, chronic pain, or a neurological disorder. Would we want others to look at us as

---

73 "George Washington Carver Quotes." *AZ Quotes*. Accessed May 25, 2019. https://www.azquotes.com/author/2580-George_Washington_Carver.

only being weak or vulnerable? Would we not appreciate those who treated us as complete persons who possess great strength because of our challenges? Surely we would want to be dignified in our circumstances, not dehumanized.

The process of considering how we would like to be treated if we experienced great physical weakness or difficult circumstances can change us. We might become more likely to look at those we previously considered weak as being strong. We might recognize that the strength it takes to live with a life-changing illness, to live on the streets, or to deal with the realities of older age is remarkable. By changing how we think about those living with vulnerability, our behaviours toward these individuals could morph. By interacting differently with those considered vulnerable, meaning in our lives could be enhanced.

> *Then the King will say ... "I was hungry and you fed me, I was thirsty and you gave me a drink, I was homeless and you gave me a room, I was shivering and you gave me clothes,*
>
> *I was sick and you stopped to visit, I was in prison and you came to me ... I'm telling the solemn truth: Whenever you did one of these things to someone overlooked or ignored, that was me—you did it to me."*
>
> —Matthew 25:34–36, 40 (MSG)

3.26 HELPING ONE IN CHRONIC SORROW

North Americans tend not to support people well over the long term. We assume that a psychologically healthy person has a grieving period of about one year after a death. We presume that other losses should have shorter grieving periods. If someone is struggling with a chronic illness, we may assume that this individual isn't coping, and that he or she needs to "buck up." This reflects our discomfort with the sorrow of others. *If this could happen to a friend or neighbour, it could happen to me.* "I don't know what to say!" is often an excuse for not providing support.

Just knowing about chronic sorrow may help us recognize it in friends or family members who are struggling with their significant physical illness or disability. Attentive listening to their concerns, as well as offering support that maintains their dignity, are important. For instance, nurses who work with bedridden people learn not to do everything for their patients. If an individual *can* do something, they often *want* to do it. A simple "Would you like a hand with that?" gives the patient the opportunity to perform the task or to receive the help, and this gives them dignity.

It can be helpful to elicit information from a recently disabled loved one or friend about who they are as individuals and what qualities they're particularly proud of. This can be a springboard to a conversation about how he could use those qualities in a different kind of work than he once performed. If his disability prevents him from returning to work as a health care provider, could he express his intelligence and care for others in another profession, such as psychology? This may help the individual partially bridge the gap between his identity and his physical disability.

This type of questioning should always be gentle and only offered after attentive listening and with the greatest respect. The discussion may simply sow seeds for further thought—options this individual hadn't considered. After her diving accident that rendered her a quadriplegic, Joni Eareckson Tada—a well-known American speaker, artist, and disability advocate—was initially offended when an occupational therapist suggested she draw with a pencil in her mouth. When this professional told her that the ability is first and foremost in her mind rather than her hands, she gave it a try. The results were beautiful paintings and drawings that no one would know came from working with an instrument in her mouth, and they led to a ministry of speaking and advocacy.

The ones we come alongside may never experience these types of results, but our careful listening and, when appropriate, respectful suggestions of possibilities might enable them to find meaning in the dirt.

3.27 AVOIDING RUMINATION ABOUT THE PAST

When we go through difficult times, it's easy to fall into a pattern of rumination about the past. We may ruminate about choices made years ago—perhaps failing to apply for university or college, or choosing unsuitable work positions. We may dwell on poor financial decisions made when we were younger, or a relationship we let go of because we were afraid to enter marriage. Regret may seep into our souls and, at times, choke us. This is an unhealthy pile of dirt to sit in!

While it's true that we can't always undo decisions made in the past, rumination doesn't better our current lives; in fact, we can become mired in this thinking and fail to recognize the blessings of our daily lives. Not only do we fail to recognize what God has and continues to give us, but we may resent the Lord for our past, or feel bitterness toward others who seem to have had an easier lot in life. This shuts down a positive relationship with God and others who could enrich our lives. Continuing in these patterns can sully our future. Please note: rumination is not simply an activity but a *way of being* that infects the whole person. "I regret that I didn't do ___" can easily become, "I've wasted my life!"

To escape this, we must recognize the blessings of God and seek out avenues of meaning in our lives. We need to discover ways to make an impact, to right a wrong, to make the world a better place. Finding and making meaning becomes an antidote for rumination about the past and a means to break unhealthy patterns of thought. Some individuals seek to find meaning in the very areas that once were problematic. For instance, those who "lost" many years to addictions may further their education and then work with those who are addicted. Others seek causes that resonate with their personalities; for example, individuals who have always loved animals may work or volunteer in animal shelters. The very act of giving to others, particularly individuals or animals who have experienced hardship or trauma, can infuse their lives with deep meaning.

The process of finding and maintaining meaning in life derails the destructive patterns of thought that are focused upon rumination and regret.[74] The Apostle Paul, in speaking of his life before He became a Christ-follower (and for which he certainly had regret), said, *"Forgetting what is behind and straining toward what is ahead ..."* (Philippians 3:13b).

---

[74] The next meditation in this section examines dealing with regrets.

3.28 Dealing with Regrets

In the previous meditation, we wrote about avoiding rumination—that "chewing of the cud" of regrets.[75] This causes difficulties in a life of meaning. If you haven't read that one, you may wish to do so first.

We all have regrets—areas of our lives that we wish had been different. Sometimes we regret something that happened to us, either beyond our control or as a result of our actions. Other times we made decisions because we had few choices: not being accepted into one plan of study may have led to choosing to forego university altogether, and we may later grieve this.

Another issue with regrets is becoming more problematic in our society: too many choices. Many people find themselves frozen into inaction because they're overwhelmed with the fear of making a bad decision.

Let's consider how to deal with regrets, both mentally and spiritually. It's vital to realize that choosing one path negates another, at least at that point in time. The idea that we can have it all is erroneous. Part of the maturity of adulthood is recognizing this and coming to grips with it. Many an adult has made disastrous decisions because of mid-life crises, trying to recapture the past (and lost youth) by making poor decisions

---

75 *Merriam-Webster Dictionary*, s.v. "Ruminate," accessed August 8, 2019, https://www.merriam-webster.com/dictionary/ruminate.

financially and relationally. Recognizing that our choices limit us gives us permission to let go of fanciful thinking: "If only I had ____."

For the unfixable regrets, think through the decisions made. Generally, we make choices based upon the best information we have, but we're not infallible.[76] We can over-estimate positive aspects or under-estimate negative ones. Or we may not have sufficient information in the first place. Hence, we need to forgive ourselves (see "Grace Toward Ourselves") and, if possible, reframe some of our thinking. For instance, when a marriage is regretted, individuals often will say, "But from this union has come three beautiful children!" This is healthy.

Where we have made choices that have hurt others and God, it's beneficial to our own mental and spiritual health to ask forgiveness and make restitution with people and to seek God's forgiveness.

Recognize that much good can come from that which has not been good. A redemptive thread runs through the scriptures, where God brings forth good out of that which is not good (Romans 8:28). In the long run, He works all things into His plans and purposes, even the evil He despises (see Genesis 50:20, TLB). It's in the difficult things that we connect most meaningfully with others; this too brings meaning.

76   Art Markman, "Why Are You Often Disappointed with Choices?" *Psychology Today*, March 7, 2018, https://www.psychologytoday.com/us/blog/ulterior-motives/201803/why-are-you-often-disappointed-choices.

3.29 The Work of Forgiveness: Regular Planting Necessary

Forgive our sins, just as we have forgiven those who did wrong to us.

—Matthew 6:12 (ERV)

Forgiveness is a central teaching within Christianity. We are instructed to forgive, as God in Christ has so freely forgiven us. (While directives may seem limiting, the commandments of the Bible are intended for our good, and following them brings great freedom.) "To forgive is to set a prisoner free and discover that the prisoner was you," said Lewis Smedes.[77]

For the small offenses of life, forgiveness is relatively easy. It involves the letting go of an offense, not holding something against someone. But for major wounds, a more comprehensive concept is necessary. For this, we love Lewis Smedes' understanding. He said that we know we have begun the cooperative work with God in the process of forgiveness when we can:

- See again the humanity of the person who has hurt us;
- Relinquish our right to revenge;

---

77   "Forgiveness Quotes." *Goodreads*. Accessed July 31, 2019. https://www.goodreads.com/quotes/tag/forgiveness?page=3.

93

- Wish that person some modicum of good in their life.[78]

Forgiveness is a *co-operative work with God*; the One full of grace is also full of truth (John 1:14). He *knows* the wounding received and doesn't ask us to minimize or forget it. And He is our helper. "Oh Lord, help me forgive!" is a God-honouring prayer. Forgiveness is a process, "a direction, not perfection," goes the popular saying. In that direction, we continue to work with the situation in our own hearts and minds. Some people seek counselling for their own healing; others conduct research into the specific way they were hurt (for instance, seeking information about family violence when one has been abused).[79] It may take years to achieve the three criteria of Smedes' definition. Sometimes, years after a grievous wounding, a person may find that they understand more about life's challenges and human brokenness, and then forgiveness comes more easily. This process is called "deferred empathy."[80]

With ongoing intent to forgive, prayers asking God for help to do so, and a search for understanding and healing for the violation incurred, we can be sure that the Lord will bring us to where we need to be. Living this way—quickly forgiving small offenses and working together with the Lord, our helper, on the big ones—lets us plant and replant good seeds where the ground may have otherwise become barren.

---

78 Lewis B. Smedes, *The Art of Forgiving* (New York, NY: Ballentine Books, 1996), 34. Please note that these points are a paraphrase of Smedes' descriptions.

79 Please note that forgiveness does not mean restored relationship. This and other thorny issues in forgiveness will be tackled in Section Four: "Weeding the Garden."

80 Mary Gunther, "Deferred Empathy: A Construct with Implications for the Mental Health of Older Adults," *Issues in Mental Health Nursing* 29, no. 9 (2008): 1029–1040.

3.30 LIFT UP YOUR HEART AND VOICE: THE DISCIPLINE OF SINGING

Words make you think. Music makes you feel. A song makes you feel a thought.[81]

—Yip Harburg

Sing songs from your heart to Christ. Sing praises over everything, any excuse for a song to God the Father in the name of our Master, Jesus Christ.

—Ephesians 5:19–20 (MSG)

S inging is a part of the universal human experience. We sing when we're happy; we sing along to our favourite radio station in the car on our way to work; we hum a tune as we work in the home; and we explode in wordless joy when something good happens. Oh, how wonderful it is when singing is the expression of the *"cup* [that] *overflows"* (Psalm 23:5b)!

The scriptures speak much about singing. The psalmists sang often for joy and exhorted others to sing also (Exodus 15:21; Psalm 13:6, 30:4). Why is this so? In light of the Ephesians 5 passage, one might conclude that God needs the praise, that perhaps He's narcissistic and demands that we recognize His greatness. Nothing could be further from the truth; we're

---

81 "Singing Quotes." *Goodreads.* Accessed July 14, 2019. https://www.goodreads.com/quotes/tag/singing.

encouraged to sing because *we* need to! According to Harburg, singing connects the mind and the emotions. Words that are put to tune and committed to memory stay with us and often come back to us at points of need, bringing comfort, peace, and hope.

In the stresses of life, the truths about life—from the scriptures and healthy perspectives—can elude us. Singing to the Lord helps us remember that the God who loves us unconditionally is caring for us, and nothing in our lives escapes His notice (Matthew 6:25–34). We can *feel* the truth, not just think it, which is a powerful help when anxiety is knocking at the door.

In Ephesians 5, we're encouraged to make up our own songs to the Lord. One may think that on-the-spot composing is only for professional songwriters, but to follow the direction of this verse brings life back into perspective. To sing to the Lord is to recognize His lordship; it helps us entrust ourselves to Him and causes us to be creative in our expressions of worship. Even those who are shy (and not musically gifted) can do this when they're alone!

This discipline brings us back to sources of meaning in life—our God, the blessings we have received, the truths that anchor us—and the singing itself can add to life's beauty.

Those who wish to sing always find a song.[82]
—Swedish Proverb

Sing and make music from your heart to the Lord.
—Ephesians 5:19b

82   Ibid.

3.31 SILENCE: SHH!

... in quietness and in confidence shall be your strength...

—Isaiah 30:15 (KJV)

In the silence of the heart God speaks. If you face God in prayer and silence, God will speak to you. ... Souls of prayer are souls of great silence.[83]

—Mother Teresa

It's commonly recognized that silence is absent from our daily lives. Many of us upon getting into our cars or entering our homes automatically turn on the radio or CD player or television. Even when going to sleep, some people have the television on as background noise. Most people keep their ears tuned to possible phone notifications. What's behind this obsession to fill every waking moment with noise?

We wonder if our fear of silence comes from unrest in our souls, or a lack of peace in our minds. Noise from the television

---

83   Mother Teresa, *In the Heart of the World: Thoughts, Stories and Prayers* (Novato, CA: New World Library, 2010), 142. Though Mother Teresa is now recognized by the Roman Catholic Church as "Saint Teresa of Calcutta," more people recognize her with matriarchal title, so we have used that one.

or music temporarily quells that unrest. While these mediums can be useful and positive (music can change our mood and induce a peaceful state), we should ask ourselves why we cannot rest in silence. What drives our need for distraction?

Various scriptures (e.g. Isaiah 30:15; Psalm 46:10) suggest that strength is garnered through silence, through stillness. Mother Teresa stated that silence is necessary to experience God through prayer. Silence affords us opportunity to think about our relationship with God, our lives, and the world in an unencumbered way. Meaningful strength is gleaned when, in silence, we consider how God has helped us in the past, is currently involved with us, and will remain present with us for the rest of our lives. Our faith isn't based upon a hoped-for result but on God's character and presence: *"Be still and know that [He] is God"* (Psalm 46:10). In the New American Standard Bible "be still" is rendered *"Cease striving,"* which is footnoted as "let go" and "relax."[84] This type of stillness only comes when we take some action (attempt to be quiet) and seek to trust Him. When we can't, in our own strength, do this, it's always appropriate to ask the Lord for help.

"The Lord is in his holy temple; let all the earth be silent before him" (Habakkuk 2:20). Making it a habit to "face God in prayer" during times of rest produces a quietness in us that helps us experience that rest in difficult circumstances.

---

84 *New American Standard Bible*, (NY: Collins Publishers, 1975), 545.

SECTION FOUR

WEEDING

INTRO TO SECTION FOUR

Weeding is not a pleasant task for many gardeners! Without it, though, there won't be a good crop. This section deals with adversities in our lives that either reveal the needs (problems within our own character) or spread weeds (such as disillusionment and resentment) into the garden of our lives. In this portion of our book, we look at some of these challenges and the productive work that can happen if we handle them well. As Jesus remarked in the parable of the sower, a crop that grows up in weedy soil is *"strangled by the weeds"* (Matthew 13:7, MSG). More than one sincere individual has had the life (that which is good and brings forth fruit) strangled in them because they didn't recognize the need to weed the soil of their life, or they chose not to. If our lives are to be meaningful and produce a good harvest, the heart must weed the soil.

4.1 MEANING IN ADVERSITY

Most of us don't relish adversity. We loathe the misfortunes that prevent us from doing what we want to do, that alter how we view the world, or threaten to overtake us. We feel out of control, afraid, confused about how to respond, and often *very alone*.

There can be great meaning in adversity, however. Perhaps the difference between those who weather well through adversity and those who don't is in how they view their challenges. As noted by the late psychiatrist and writer Elisabeth Kubler-Ross:

> The most beautiful people we have known are those who have known defeat, known suffering, known struggle, known loss, and have found their way out of the depths. These persons have an appreciation, a sensitivity, and an understanding of life that fills them with compassion, gentleness, and a deep loving concern. Beautiful people do not just happen.[85]

Those who endure adversity well may choose to trust God for their circumstances, particularly those that they can't

---

85 "Adversity Quotes." *Goodreads*. Accessed May 27, 2019. https://www.goodreads.com/quotes/tag/adversity.

control. They believe that difficult circumstances come to all people and refuse to buy into the idea that they have received a bad rap in life. They also reject fatalistic beliefs that they can't do anything helpful to cope during challenging situations. They don't try to cope using prevalent cultural responses to adversity, such as denial or an extremely positive attitude (another form of denial). Constructive coping methods may include being honest about how one is feeling, periodic distraction, exercise, seeking support from trusted others, as well as faith in God's *good* presence in their circumstances. It also involves being alert to what one is learning during such a period and how one is changing. To use psychologist Susan David's terms, they exercise "emotional agility" rather than "emotional rigidity."[86]

In the process of responding constructively to adversity over a period of time, these individuals change for the better. As Kubler-Ross explains, they appreciate life and are more compassionate and gentle with others. While these individuals admit that the adversity was arduous and they're grateful that life has improved, they also acknowledge meaning in the adversity: they have changed for the better, and they look at life differently. "Life's beauty is inseparable from its fragility," said Dr. Susan David. "Discomfort is the price of admission to a meaningful life."[87]

---

86 For an excellent explanation of these concepts, please see Susan David. "The Gift and Power of Emotional Courage." *TED Talk*. February 20, 2018. https://www.bing.com/videos/search?q=susan+david%27s+t-ed+talk&&view=detail&mid=A09EEB06AAD801906B93A09EE-B06AAD801906B93&rvsmid=081F40C41E5AC5472C02081F40C41E5A C5472C02&FORM=VDRVRV.

87 Ibid.

4.2 BOUNDARIES NEEDED: WEEDY SOIL IN HELPING OTHERS

When our meaning-making involves others, we experience many joys, but we also encounter areas with thistles. One such area is that of boundaries. Boundaries are the fences around the gardens of our lives that distinguish where each person ends and begins; they protect us and others.[88]

In some areas of helping, the boundaries are clear. This would include avoiding physical relationships with those we're helping. Other aspects of maintaining boundaries are less straightforward, such as emotional boundaries. For some, helping others can come out of *their* need to feel good about themselves. This isn't completely wrong, as helping others can be a means of fulfilling their vocation to serve. However, when this help becomes more about the helper than the one being helped, a boundary is crossed. This becomes evident when the helper becomes angry when his help is rejected, ("After all I've done for him!"), or trusted others in the helper's life question his motivation.

At this point, some questions need to be asked. If we are helping, are we helping others because *we* need to feel good about ourselves? Are our actions impeding others from

---

88 We are indebted to Henry Cloud and John Townsend for the concepts in this meditation. See *Boundaries*, updated ed. (Grand Rapids, MI: Zondervan, 2017).

fulfilling their personal responsibilities? Are we neglecting other areas of our lives because we're spending so much time with this one individual or project? "Yes" responses indicate that we're using people to fulfill our needs, which violates their boundaries, even if this isn't the intent.

Those who need help can cross boundaries too, such as a phone call in the middle of the night regarding matters that could be discussed the next day, or anger toward the helper when she isn't always available to help. Another indication of crossed boundaries could be that the helper is feeling pressured and coerced.

The soil of our lives can be effectively weeded when we understand boundaries and are self-aware. For the helper, taking a step back when he becomes aware that he's helping for the wrong reasons, or when he's feeling used, is wise. The one being helped can and should also say "no" when they sense they have lost control in the help being offered.

When we recognize unhealthy patterns within ourselves and take measures to deal with them, we weed the garden of our souls and prevent others from planting their weeds in our gardens.

> Compassionate people ask for what they need. They say no when they need to, and when they say yes, they mean it. They're compassionate because their boundaries keep them out of resentment.[89]
>
> —Brené Brown

---

89   "Boundaries Quotes." *Goodreads*. Accessed July 18, 2019. https://www. goodreads.com/quotes/tag/boundaries?page=3.

4.3 Chronic Sorrow: When the Losses Don't End

In the early 1960s, the term "chronic sorrow" was used to describe a normal psychological response that parents felt when a child was born with a developmental disability.[90] This term has continued to be used in this way, as well as in any situation where a disability or illness in the child is ongoing. The illness or condition is chronic—unending, constant, unabating. Because of this, the parents' sorrow is also interminable. *How will I manage to care for my child as I get older? What will happen to him/her when I die?* For these parents, the losses feel never-ending.

The scope of this term has now broadened to include adults who experience physical illness, disability, or injury that changes what they can do—for example, adults who now need a wheelchair or are homebound. However, their sorrow goes beyond their lost skills to their actual sense of identity.[91] Perhaps the illness or disability has developed over time, and the adult remembers a time when things were different. A woman with macular degeneration may have been a prolific

---

90 Simon Olshansky, "Chronic Sorrow: A Response to Having a Mentally Defective Child," *Social Casework* (April 1962): 190–193. Please note: the title of this article reflects the terminology of the day (1962) and would not be used by us nor in public discourse today.

91 Kaethe Weingarten, "Sorrow: A Therapist's Reflection on the Inevitable and the Unknowable," *Family Process* 51 (2012): 440–455.

reader, which was a source of identity, meaning, and joy. But now, her ever-diminishing eyesight severely limits her reading. Understandably, she feels chronic sorrow. She mourns the loss of what she had and was, and wonders what she'll do for the rest of her life. She worries about the future. So human!

If you find yourself in such a circumstance, may we encourage you to begin to see yourself as more than how you identified yourself in the past? In a society that emphasizes accomplishment, we learn to be *doers*—we identify ourselves by what we can do. However, a powerful understanding at the beginning of life (parents with infants) and at the end of life (palliative care) is that we are inherently valuable because we *are*. With that understanding of our inherent worth, we can begin to look for new sources of activity and meaning in life. Individuals who have overcome great losses to find meaning and contribute to society are considered "inspirational," and rightly so. For some, the meaning they find in the dirt—the overwhelming challenge—can be greater than when life was easier.

4.4 GRACE MISAPPLIED (GRACE, PART FOUR)

Within this book, we have looked at grace from God, grace from/toward others, and grace toward ourselves. But at times grace can be misapplied. Sometimes saying "I forgive you" isn't appropriate, or not enough.

Within religious circles, brushing things under the carpet, forgetting about abuses, refusing to hold someone accountable for their actions, are often mistaken for grace. For example, an abused wife can extend the grace of forgiveness to her abuser, but there still needs to be a reckoning for the husband's actions. This may mean a jail sentence, anger management courses, or separation from the family, whether temporarily or permanently. The irresponsible adult child may need money from her parents again, but money given indiscriminately may be benevolence misapplied. In the application of grace, the true needs of the person appealing for grace, as well as the needs of others, should be taken into account.

Jesus was full of grace and truth (John 1:14). While he forgave and dignified people who had moral failings, he also directed them to "*sin no more*" (John 8:11, KJV). Within society and societal organizations, including the family, the broader unit must be considered when applying grace to individual actions. While forgiveness is a great blessing, consequences for wrong-doing/irresponsibility are also needed. In this way, the one who did wrong may learn, and the one(s) who experienced the wrong, as well as the greater whole, may be rightly cared for.

4.5 SPACIOUS LIVES (PART TWO): THE CHALLENGE OF TENDING TO OUR INNER WORLD

What lies behind us and what lies before us are tiny matters compared with what lies within us.[92]

—Ralph Waldo Emerson

L iving spacious lives means tending to our inner selves. It has been said that in modern times, we live soul-less lives,[93] rushing to and fro, constantly connected to our wireless devices. With our brains continually engaged, we run from our inner selves. When we do this, we become impoverished; we have less to give to others, and we do not know who we are.

Why are we running? Partly, we believe, we fear what we may find within. Sometimes, through the words that have been said to us, poisonous weeds have been planted into the soil of our souls. *You're no good! You'll never amount to anything!* Our experiences may have involved wounds inflicted upon us by an abuser, also leaving us with weeds of shame. We may be

---

92 "Ralph Waldo Emerson Quotes." *Goodreads.* Accessed: June 1, 2019. https://www.goodreads.com/quotes/15579-what-lies-behind-us-and-what-lies-before-us-are.

93 In 2004, Pope John Paul II warned about a "soulless vision of life in America." See "Pope Worries About Soulless America." *NBC News.* Accessed June 25, 2019. http://www.nbcnews.com/id/5084947/ns/world_news/t/pope-worries-about-soulless-life-america/#.XRPfondFy8A.

running from our own actions or wrongs we have committed against others.

Some psychologists distinguish between shame (*I am bad*) and guilt (*I have done something bad*), and we need to know the difference between the two and deal with each differently. Dealing with shame involves weeding the lies of our minds and planting truth. Where there is guilt, there are ways to deal with this, such as asking forgiveness of the person we have hurt. If laws have been broken, we may face legal consequences. Any religion with a concept of sin includes a way of dealing with it. Dealing with shame and guilt can bring life to the garden of the mind and quiet a restless soul.[94]

Tending to the inner self means getting used to being quiet and listening to one's soul. This can be done in the minutes (or sometimes hours) before sleep comes by letting the memories of the day sift through our minds and asking forgiveness from God for attitudes we regret. (And then let go of them—weeding again!) We can also give thanks for the joys of the day. It can also be a time to listen to the sounds of the night—a bird's call, a train's whistle in the distance, the snores of the dog sleeping by the bed.

The garden of the mind is to be a place of peace and joy. By dealing with the weeds (painful places) of our souls and planting good crops, we create the spaciousness of the inner life. Tending to this makes life rich.

---

94   Please note: a counsellor or pastor can be invaluable in helping one deal with shame and/or guilt.

4.6 "It's Hard to Grow Old!" The Importance of Meaning in Aging

Our mom often said to us, "It's hard to grow old, you know!" Indeed, it is a challenging time of life, and many people fear aging. Societal discourse that emphasizes youth and re-maining young (through plastic surgery or other means) is powerful. People dread aging, not only because it brings phys-ical changes and a closer proximity to death, but also because of society's devaluation of older adults. It doesn't matter how many commercials one sees on television of individuals aging vibrantly, the fact that millions of dollars are spent annually to stave off the outward signs of aging reveal how society—in-cluding those who are getting older—feels. How should aging individuals respond?

A balanced response should acknowledge the challenges (changes in health, deaths of family members and/or friends) but also include an optimistic look forward to the opportu-nities for creativity and meaning. Research has shown that adults who are creative, particularly between the ages of fif-ty-five and seventy-five, experience the best years of their lives.[95] Further, aging adults who engage in meaningful

---

95   Gene Cohen. "The Creativity and Aging Study: The Impact of Profes-sionally Conducted Cultural Programs on Older Adults," *Scribd*. Ac-cessed April 19, 2019. https://www.scribd.com/document/133045514/Gene-Cohen-Creativity-and-Aging.

activities, such as helping others through paid or volunteer work, praying for others, and serving in organizations within their community, find fulfillment. Not only are they able to unite their passions with their time and activities, but their days also have some structure. Structure to our days, in addition to meaningful activity, decreases boredom. In one seminar we conducted a number of years ago on transitions and making meaning, a lovely older woman approached us and exclaimed, "Now I know what my problem is! I am bored!" This realization led her to make changes in her life, and subsequently, she experienced greater meaning.

Teach us to number our days and recognize how few they are; help us to spend them as we should.

—Psalm 90:12 (TLB)

4.7 MISCONCEPTIONS ABOUT FORGIVENESS

We focused on forgiveness in the previous section, but we felt that we needed to round out the topic by discussing misconceptions regarding forgiveness. Within Christian doctrine and practice, there have been few thornier patches of ground.

First is the misconception that forgiveness and trust are the same. Not so. "Forgiveness is granted; trust is earned," states the common saying. A husband who has had an affair cannot expect the unquestioning trust of his spouse; it will take significant time to rebuild trust within the relationship. In some circumstances, the relationship is best severed. A woman beaten up by her boyfriend should not, under the guise of "forgiveness," be counselled to get back into the relationship. The same could be said for those who are beaten up by spouses.[96]

Second, the idea that to forgive means there should not be consequences is misguided. In the case of a law broken,

---

96   There are many sources that would agree with us (see, for example, Lewis B. Smedes, *The Art of Forgiving* [New York, NY: Ballentine Books, 1996]). Certainly, in non-religious counselling, this has been the case for decades. However, in conservative church circles, there are still many who believe that a marriage relationship must be preserved. Hence, we include this point here.

authorities must be contacted (see Romans 13:1–5). The vulnerable must be protected within the family and within the church.

A third misconception is the idea that people must forgive instantly. Insisting that deeply wounded people forgive quickly re-violates them.[97] Insisting that people say the words "I forgive you" is yet another violation. A wounded person is grieving a number of losses: innocence, a relationship, a hoped-for future, a job, or financial security, to name a few. They will need to grieve and, in time, forgive.

Finally, forgiveness doesn't mean that one cannot tell their story.[98] While not every setting is suitable for telling a story of violation, a deeply wounded person should not be told that they are "unforgiving" for speaking truthfully about what they've experienced and their struggles in dealing with their pain. (This is one reason why counselling is helpful for one who has suffered great wounding. Here a person can tell and retell their story.)

This is important information for those who have been significantly hurt and for those who help others. If we want our assistance to be meaningful, we need to understand the dynamics of relationships and have a basic grasp of societal issues, such as domestic violence, so that we're not guilty of introducing thorns into others' gardens.

---

97 Myrla Seibold, "When the Wounding Runs Deep: Encouragement for Those on the Road to Forgiveness," in *Care for the Soul*, eds. Mark R. McMinn and Timothy R. Phillips (Downer's Grove, IL: InterVarsity Press, 2001), 294–308.

98 Ibid.

4.8 OH, THE UNFAIRNESS OF LIFE!

Children often respond to situations by exclaiming, "That's not fair!" Their reaction may be based upon disappointment over unmet desires. As adults, we often have a similar response to life, and for good reason. Life truly is not fair.

Beyond disappointment when life doesn't turn out as expected, we contend with tragedies such as the untimely deaths of loved ones, violence, abuse of children and vulnerable people, and war or poverty. Decades ago, Rabbi Harold Kushner wrote a book, *When Bad Things Happen to Good People.*[99] This book was an enormous success because it addressed the tormenting questions we face when battered by unfairness and tragedy.[100]

While there's nothing wrong with exclaiming that life isn't fair, we also need to recognize that those of us living in the Western world enjoy many privileges that people in developing nations don't experience. We generally have more medical services, educational opportunities, food, and luxuries.[101] In this

---

99   Harold Kushner, *When Bad Things Happen to Good People* (New York, NY: Random House, 1981).

100 Rabbi Kushner's theological response to the "why" questions does not satisfy everyone, however.

101 We do recognize, however, that in parts of the Western world, such as in the Canadian north, people do not enjoy the amenities that Canadians in large urban centres often do.

sense, life's unfairness works for us and sets our discontent in a broader context.

How do we respond to the unfairness of life in a meaningful way? First, we must grieve the losses/tragedies of our lives; this can be a lengthy process. We also may be helped by extending our gaze beyond this world. This life is not the final chapter; heaven will bring great joy and purpose that will last eternally. When we can't muster the strength to turn our gaze toward God, we can seek and rely upon the prayers of others to strengthen us. It's valuable to belong to a Christian community that can circle the wagons around us when we're vulnerable!

We can also seek ways to bring meaning to the unfairness and tragedy we've faced. Volunteering for an organization that addresses how our loved ones suffered and died (such as a cancer society) can be very meaningful. Those with substantial monetary resources may start a foundation to honour the memory of their loved one. In ongoing acts like these, the memory of one's loved one is kept alive, and those who mourn gain a sense that the death was not in vain.

Finally, we can seek to address the injustices in other parts of the world, such as poverty or the lack of education for girls, through financial support or short-term volunteer work. In this way, the ground of unfairness can yield meaning in our lives and in the lives of others.

4.9 The Challenge of Transition and Change

It's only after you've stepped outside your comfort zone that you begin to change, grow, and transform.[102]

—Roy T. Bennett

While not all people struggle with transition and change, many do, and for good reason. Bridges describes the process of transition as leaving individuals in a "confusing nowhere of in-betweenness."[103] This "in-betweenness" may leave us anxious, fearful, and not knowing who we are in the world.

How are "transition" and "change" different? Bridges suggests that transition is more than just change and includes the psychological processes in adapting to the change.[104] In our experiences, some individuals refuse to transition when faced by challenges, whether this involves embracing developmental milestones or dealing with tragedies within their lives. The psychological discomfort is just too much. Paradoxically,

---

102 "Change Quotes." *Goodreads*. Accessed June 17, 2019. https://www.goodreads.com/quotes/tag/change.

103 William Bridges, *Transitions: Making Sense of Life's Changes* (Reading, MA: Da Capo Press, 1980), 47.

104 Bridges. *Transitions*.

117

a failure to transition may become a transition in and of itself, as it changes a life course significantly.[105]

Changes and transitions can be experienced as the weed-infested soil of adversity in making meaning. When we experience a traumatic change or transition, such as the death of a spouse, a divorce, or the loss of a job we loved, we may question the meaning of life. This is understandable, as our life paradigm may be shattered. We may also put meaning-making activities on hold while we deal with our grief and loss. This is also reasonable. However, at some point we might want to consider returning to the activities that have brought us meaning. Not only do they occupy time and bring a modicum of normalcy to our lives when our world has been turned upside down, but being with others and hearing their stories (especially when they have weathered similar situations) may bring comfort and courage. By recognizing that others have survived such traumatic events, we can believe that we will also get through the heart-wrenching challenge, and that someday we may be able to help others. That can bring meaning to a death or trauma that seems meaningless.

Whether the change is seen as positive or negative, transition is the ground for growth, and weeding the soil of our garden during difficult times can produce an excellent harvest of character—endurance, strength, sensitivity, humility. Our response to these periods of our lives makes the difference between the misshaping or the healthy formation of the soul.

> All humans change. Development is our life. Transition, in labor, is the most painful time. Without change, there's no growth.[106]
>
> —Mimi Kennedy

---

105 Lane and Reed. *Older Adults.*

106 "Transitions Quote." *BrainyQuote.* Accessed July 19, 2019. www. brainyquote.com/quotes/mimi_kennedy_702027?src=t_transition.

4.10 TOO EXHAUSTED
TO MAKE MEANING

At times in our lives we're too exhausted to engage in making meaning. This may come at times when work is particularly challenging, when children are going through a rough
time at school, or when older parents are failing and needing
additional support. Understandably, we may withdraw from
some of our meaning-making commitments, such as volunteering at church or with community organizations. But what
happens when we're too emotionally or physically exhausted
to engage in disciplines such as prayer, reading scripture, or
other activities that feed our souls? Many sincere Christians
feel badly about this, thinking they're letting God down.

When we're feeling exhausted, we should visit a doctor to
rule out illness. We also need to take a serious look at where
we can decrease stress in our lives. This involves examining
more than our activities; it also entails taking a careful look
at our approaches to stressful situations. For example, do we
feel that family members cannot give the quality of care to an
aging parent that we can, so we refuse their help? Are we re-
luctant to make use of services, such as day programs for aging
adults? These services would give us time to relax or go out
with friends as a way of restoring our energy and souls. If we
have trouble giving ourselves permission to curtail duties, we
can ask trusted friends for advice on where we can trim the
demands in our lives. We can also ask others to pray for us. We

can even ask God the Holy Spirit to pray in us and for us. How amazing is this? To think that God would pray for us![107]

Understanding that seasons of extreme stress are usually time-limited, we can reassure ourselves that our focus on making meaning will return, including making meaning through spiritual disciplines such as prayer and scripture reading. This may help assuage some guilt we unwittingly place upon ourselves. We can also understand that God is not disappointed in us. Psalm 103:14 reassures us, *"for he knows how we are formed, he remembers that we are dust."* Rather than an insult, this is a relief. In response to this passage of scripture, it has been said, "You can't put a whole lot of responsibility on dust now, can you." Phew!

---

107 While some translations speak of the Holy Spirit praying in us, *The Message* speaks of the Spirit praying both in us and for us. *"He does our praying in and for us, making prayer out of our wordless sighs, our aching groans"* (Romans 8:27, emphasis ours).

4.11 WHEN OUR BEST IS NOT GOOD ENOUGH

M any of us have found ourselves in situations where we
think, *I did everything I could, but my best was not good
enough!* This exclamation of frustration may be in response to
not receiving a promotion that we worked hard for, or it may
be a reaction to a failed business, when exceedingly long hours
weren't sufficient to keep our dream afloat. It may also come
when we have tried to extend love and support to a family
member, but despite our ardent attempts over a lengthy period
of time, the relative simply would not reciprocate our generos-
ity of spirit.

It may be tempting to sink into feelings of depression or
despair. *How could my best not be good enough?* Perhaps even
more disturbing: *If my best isn't good enough, how can I compete
in this world and/or maintain meaning in life?*

Grieving the loss of a dream or anticipated outcome is
normal and healthy. So is expressing our frustrations and wor
ries to trusted others. As demoralizing as failed dreams or un-
anticipated outcomes can be, however, they offer us a chance
to take stock of our lives. What gives our life meaning? Is it
possible that the dreams we pursued were not in line with what
affords the most meaning in life? Did the unrealized dreams
pull us too far away from family, friends, faith, or causes we
believe in?

The purpose of this reflection isn't to make us feel worse about ourselves but to bring meaning out of otherwise devastating situations. When we can learn through a negative situation, we're afforded the opportunity to reframe or re-evaluate how we view the circumstance. Not only does it become less devastating, perhaps improving our view of ourselves, but we may consider putting greater efforts into the work or relationships that mean the most to us. The impact of this can be profound. It's not uncommon to hear individuals with life-changing illnesses state that while they wouldn't have chosen it, the sickness powerfully changed how they live their lives. They admit that it took an intense situation to jolt them out of their previous ways of being, and surprising to them, the changes have improved their lives markedly.

The challenge for us is to engage not only in reflection upon difficult circumstances but also to take inventory of what brings us meaning. Following this, we can make changes that may bring lasting richness to our lives. Socrates said, "The unexamined life is not worth living,"[108] and while this may seem like an overstatement, to live a meaningful life requires the ability to take stock of our circumstances and sometimes make course alterations. While our best may not have been good enough, *the* best may be yet to come.

---

108 "Socrates Quotes." *BrainyQuote*. Accessed July 29, 2019. https://www.brainyquote.com/quotes/socrates_101168.

4.12 HOW DO WE RESPOND MEANINGFULLY TO THE TEARS OF OTHERS?

If one is involved in bringing meaning to others, they will certainly be faced with the tears of others from time to time. It can be difficult to know how to respond when others weep. We may be fearful because we don't want to say or do the "wrong" thing. As stated in Section Two, tears may have been unacceptable in our family of origin (or unacceptable for our gender within our family). Our discomfort with weeping may also be due to the use of tears to manipulate. A child that cries to get her own way is part of the immaturity of that age and stage. The adults in her life work with her to regulate the emotions and to think outside of herself. An adult who uses tears to manipulate is exploiting others. This meditation is not about responding to those type of tears.

Responding well to the sincere tears of others involves both skill and presence. The empathic presence of the observer of the tears honours the one who is crying. Sometimes, no words are necessary. A hand on the shoulder or the provision of some tissue may be all that the sorrowful person needs. It's okay—often good—to be silent for a period of time. (Remember that the crying person's tears are sacred.) But often something needs to be said. Social worker Brené Brown, in her humorous video clip on empathy, suggests this: "I don't even know what to say right now; I'm just so glad you told me."[109] These words acknowledge the difficulty of knowing what might be helpful to say (and in some circumstances, no words can improve the situation). Brown's response also honours the person and their emotions by letting them know that the listener feels privileged with this trust.

The expression of the sincere tears of another reveals the weeper's trust in the listener. If someone in your life chooses to share such a tender portion of their soul with you, it means they consider you to be trustworthy, understanding, and safe. This is more than a lovely compliment; it is a gift from them to you. And their sharing—via words and tears—is sacred.

When you care, listening empathetically and responding to the tears of others sensitively, you are participating in the work of the Holy Spirit, the Comforter (John 14:16, KJV), and the person who has wept has received the comfort of God through you. Amazing!

---

109 "Brené Brown on Empathy." *YouTube.*

4.13 WHEN THE WORLD BECOMES SMALL: PHYSICAL LIMITATIONS CAN IMPEDE MEANING-MAKING

There is joy in movement! The ability to move intentionally, through walking or exercising, is a wonderful thing. But what happens when our movements are limited? What if we can physically move but not drive? How does one continue to make meaning when it's impossible to get out and be involved?

While movement is a great way to ensure continued meaning, it's not the only way. Some individuals keep meaningful connections with others through technology. This facilitates support for the individual experiencing challenges with movement but also allows them to *give* support, which is vital to meaning.

There is another way, however. We knew of a woman who was almost blind and deaf and confined to a wheelchair in her long-term care facility. A significant part of her meaning was found in her relationship with God and others. Previously a parish nurse, she would pray much—for people around the world and for those right beside her within the facility. If someone was dying alone on her floor, the nurses would bring her into that person's room (with that resident's permission, of course), and she would hold their hand and pray silently for them.

If your world seems to be getting smaller and smaller, look both *inward* and *upward*. Those who are shut-in can broaden their horizons through relationship with the One who is transcendent, beyond all limitations, and they can love others through prayer. The Apostle Paul saw the value, indeed the necessity, of this practice. He emphasized this repeatedly in his letters to the early church. We close with these examples of looking to God, as well as praying for others and oneself:

Rejoice always and delight in your faith; be unceasing and persistent in prayer; in every situation [no matter what the circumstances] be thankful and continually give thanks to God; for this is the will of God for you in Christ Jesus.

—1 Thessalonians 5:16–18 (AMP)

Don't fret or worry. Instead of worrying, pray. Let petitions and praises shape your worries into prayers, letting God know your concerns. Before you know it, a sense of God's wholeness, everything coming together for good, will come and settle you down. It's wonderful what happens when Christ displaces worry at the center of your life.

—Philippians 4:6–7 (MSG)

THE HARVEST

INTRO TO SECTION FIVE

Do you like to read the end of the book before its preceding chapters? Do you prefer to eat dessert before your vegetables? It is so human, in this broken world, to want the rewards before (or without) having done the work! But scripture and life teach us that it doesn't work that way.

Using the metaphor of dirt, the ground needs to be staked out, the soil tilled, the seeds planted, and the weeds pulled. After a time of patient tending, there will be a harvest. The harvest is both evidence of effective gardening—what your life lived meaningfully looks like and its impact upon others—as well as the reward (the satisfaction of baskets full of produce).[110] It can also be what we hope for: eternal rewards.

As so much of the harvest in any life is yet to come, this section will be shorter. But we hope that it whets your appetite.

---

110 We have not included in this metaphor situations beyond a gardener's control, such as hailstorms.

5.1 SHINING LIGHTS

Let your light shine before men in such a way that they may see your good works, and glorify your Father who is in heaven.

— Matthew 5: 16 (NASB)

Many of us have flown into a city when it's dark, and we've marvelled at its bright lights. Or perhaps we've been camping at night and seen the stars in their brilliant splendor. Lights are most noticeable when it's dark.

Jesus instructed us to shine before others in such a way that they see our lives and recognize that *God is the source* of lives that help others. Letting our lights shine should not be confused with the arrogant parading of good deeds for others to see. This type of light shines forth from the work of character formation (see Section Two). The impact of this kind of life is incredibly bright and winsome, especially when individuals don't draw attention to themselves. It's easily recognized through its response to others' accolades; praise given to one who is truly humble is received graciously, but then the subject is changed. If possible, the others' contributions are acknowledged.

An example of a shining light was (and still is) Mother Teresa. She didn't do her good works to garner applause. In fact, she worked tirelessly and with little notice for decades, until the 1960s and 1970s when she became known.[111] In all those years of toil, the rich character of love, humility, empathy, integrity, courage, strength, and tenderness was formed. When fame did come, the trappings of it were not tempting.

The work of character development written about in this book makes meaning, and it draws others to the source of those traits: God. This is part of our impact—or, more accurately, God's impact through us. Jesus said, *"I am the light of the world"* (John 8:12; 9:5). It's amazing and challenging that He would call *us* to shine in such a way as to guide others to Him! This shining light endures in our lifetime, and like Mother Teresa, it may shine forth for generations to come.

---

111 "Biography Mother Teresa." *Biography Online.* Accessed August 10, 2019. https://www.biographyonline.net/nobelprize/mother_teresa.html.

5.2 THE IMPACT OF PRAYER
UPON THE WORLD

Prayer, or talking about praying, is so common in faith circles that it often seems routine. How often have we said or heard, "I will pray for you"? We may in time tire of this phrase and think that it's too routine or perfunctory, and hence doesn't mean much.

While sometimes individuals use the act of prayer as an excuse *not* to physically help others (not to get their hands dirty), prayer is enormously powerful. Not only can we impact others in our neighbourhoods through prayer, but we can pray for others across the world! This is an incredible privilege. Sadly, we may not realize the privilege, as we may not see the results and thus conclude that our prayers weren't effective. We wonder if in eternity we may be exposed to the impact of our prayers for others across the globe. How rewarding and humbling this would be.

I (Annette) have never felt the positive effect of prayer so much as in the last number of months. With my diagnosis of metastatic cancer, Marlette has mobilized people to pray for me— not just in our home city, but across Canada. For the most part, I have felt "carried" by the prayers of others. While for months I was in shock and scared, I experienced a sense of God walking close to me, more so than what I've felt throughout my Christian life. I have been amazed by this. When individuals tell me, "I am praying for you," I can honestly respond with gratitude and mention that the prayers are felt and experienced. I am being impacted by the importance and power of prayer.

We often don't realize the importance of our prayers and may view prayer as an obligation we struggle through. Knowing that our prayers impact not just those in our community but individuals across the world should motivate us in this powerful faith discipline.

If we need just a little more motivation to change the world through prayer, we offer one last thought: Within the book of Revelation, there is indication that our prayers are collected in bowls (5:8). So valuable are our prayers to God that He stores them. Why would these prayers be of value? Here is a suggestion: Every parent keeps things that their child makes in school. At the Reed home, we kept a paper bag turkey that our son made for Thanksgiving in grade three. It wasn't until it was in tatters that we threw it away. It wasn't the quality of the turkey that mattered; it was that our son made it! Similarly, perhaps our heavenly Father keeps the "turkeys" of our prayers because we, His children, constructed them. Just a thought.

5.3 PERSONAL LEGACY: TO EACH HIS OWN

What has my life meant in this world, and how will that meaning continue after I'm gone? These are important questions that may arise in times of great stress, illness, or the death of loved ones. There also is a movement among adults, especially those who are aging, to determine what their legacy will be and how to ensure that this legacy continues after they have passed on.

What is a legacy? We know that a legacy often involves an inheritance—money that's bequeathed from one person to family members or friends. Another common understanding of legacy is consequence. Sometimes the consequence of an inheritance is devastation. For example, when one adult child receives a substantially greater inheritance than his or her siblings without just cause and explanation, or when an adult child recklessly wastes what an industrious parent worked so hard to bequeath. The intended legacy (blessing) results in devastation. This is tragic!

We are most concerned about another synonym for legacy: fruit.[112] From the garden of your life, what has been the fruit, the harvest? For some, their legacies involve children. (Remember the old expression *fruit of the womb*?) When they

---

112 *The Free Dictionary*, s.v. "Legacy," accessed August 21, 2019, https://www.freethesaurus.com/legacy.

have passed from this world, their children carry on the family name, as well as family values. Others may have worked a lifetime to build a family business, and formally passing this business on to one or more children is a dream come true.

For others, legacies involve personal commitment to societal issues. Through regular volunteerism, funds, the informal promotion of values and causes that are vital to them, society is impacted. This work is both an expression of who they are as individuals (another synonym for legacy is *footprint* [113]) and what comes from this work (the fruit, the harvest).

It's not vain to reflect upon one's life, identify themes, and consider what one's legacy will be. It's actually wise, as after one's death, things that are regrettable cannot be changed. Take time to reflect. It may be useful to discuss your desire for a legacy with trusted family members and friends, or a pastor or counsellor. They can help you identify the themes of your life and encourage you to rejoice in what is good and rectify something that's not.

The common theme in positive legacy[114] is leaving for the world something(s) of value, whether that be children, work to improve the world, or beauty. Said Vitor Belfort, "Legacy is not what I did for myself. It's what I'm doing for the next generation."[115]

---

113 *Lexico*, s.v. "Legacy," accessed August 21, 2019, https://www.lexico.com/en/synonym/legacy.

114 We use the term positive legacy here, because there are people who leave very negative legacies. They wish to be remembered and do so through criminal acts that harm many others, such as mass shootings.

115 "Legacy Quotes." *BrainyQuote*. Accessed July 30, 2019. https://www.brainyquote.com/quotes/vitor_belfort_978006?src=t_legacy.

5.4 COLLECTIVE LEGACY: THE POWER OF THE GROUP

Throughout this book, we have addressed the process of meaning-making in our own lives and through helping others. This is a lovely way to make a difference in this world. It's also possible for a group to make a collective legacy, and that harvest may be much greater than the sum of individual gardens. Why? Because of *synergy*. Synergy is "the interaction of elements that, when combined, produce a total effect that is greater than the sum of the individual elements, contributions, etc."[116] This type of legacy may bless communities; it may influence society's policies and practices at a governmental level; it may also impact other nations.

Many of us are involved in some type of community effort, through a community centre, our children's school, or a church. Others join political parties, seeking to influence the policies of their province or the nation. Often we don't consider our involvements as being significant. Let's unearth this concept. The women who prepare a luncheon after a funeral service help to facilitate the grief and the fellowship of an entire community. The men who tend to outdoor skating rinks at a community centre facilitate a hockey season for many young people, which enables them to increase in physical strength,

---

116   *Dictionary.com*, s.v. "Synergy," accessed August 22, 2019, https://www.
dictionary.com/browse/synergy?s=t.

skills, and positive personality development. In both of these examples, individuals play their role, but the combination of each individual's effort produces an effect far beyond each one's particular contribution. The possibilities of collective legacy are endless.

Consider a very interesting example that is both local and global—the Grandmothers to Grandmothers campaign. In 2006, aging grandmothers in Canada formed a grassroots response to the dire circumstances faced by grandmothers in Africa—women who were/are raising grandchildren because their adult children have died from AIDS. The Canadian grandmothers have gone to parliament to lobby the government to send AIDS medications to Africa. The movement has spread to the United States, Australia, and the United Kingdom.[117] The original Canadian group of grandmothers likely couldn't imagine that their efforts would become so widespread (synergy). This example reveals how "ordinary" (we would suggest *extraordinary*) women can collectively make a global impact through their desire to live in a meaningful way.

There are also individuals who have spent many years in the service of vulnerable others in needy areas around the globe. With their teams, they accomplish profound results, rebuilding communities torn apart through war or natural disasters.

The Apostle Paul uses the metaphor of a human body, with each part playing a role for the overall good (see Romans 12). Collective contribution! Have you considered your involvement in collective legacy?

---

117 "Grandmothers to Grandmothers Campaign." *Grandmothers to Grandmothers Campaign.* Accessed August 22, 2019, http://grandmotherscampaign.org/.

5.5 A Safe Place for Others to Dwell: You Are a Part of the Harvest

When your life is filled with meaning-making, your very self can become a safe place for others to come and spend time. While this isn't always the case (some individuals who work tirelessly for good causes can be much more comfortable in task-based activities), the character development discussed in Section Two may result in others being drawn to you. Instinctively, individuals in need feel safe, and they may seek you out. Moses said in Psalm 90:1: *"Lord, you have been our dwelling place throughout all generations."*

The Master Gardener, who has been so involved in our lives tilling the soil of character, giving us the desire and the strength to plant that which is good, and weeding out that which is not (Philippians 2:13), has been a safe place for us to dwell. From this work, the Gardener has developed within us the ability to be a safe place for others. In this way, we are a part of God's harvest; miraculously, by our very presence with others, we become part of the harvest of our own lives.

Let's switch the metaphor using (again) A.A. Milne's characters from his *Winnie the Pooh* series.

Piglet sidled up to Pooh from behind. "Pooh?" he whispered.
"Yes, Piglet?"

"Nothing," said Piglet, taking Pooh's hand. "I just wanted to be sure of you."[118]

Oh, how we can relate to Piglet! At times we have been insecure in our life circumstances, and we have felt the need to literally or metaphorically take another's hand. But here's the question: Can others be sure of you? Are you such a person? Our blessing and prayer for you is that by being a safe dwelling place for others, you will reap an abundant harvest.

118 "A.A. Milne Quotes." *Goodreads*. Accessed May 6, 2019. https://www.goodreads.com/quotes/1336-piglet-sidled-up-to-pooh-from-behind-pooh-he-whispered.

5.6 HEAVEN: PART OF THE HARVEST

There are few compelling beliefs about heaven in our culture. Our images depict it as incredibly boring: one long church service that never ends, wearing our wings and halos, riding clouds and strumming harps. The images are so bland and unappealing that folks have sometimes said they'd rather not go there!

These images are not accurate. We are counselled in scripture that in heaven we will be rewarded for the lives we have lived (Matthew 6:19–20; 2 Corinthians 3:8, 5:10; Revelation 2:23; 22:12); it will be a place of peace and joy (Romans 14:7; Revelation 22:4); there will be no sickness or death (Philippians 3:20; Revelation 21:4); and we will no longer groan with the effects of brokenness (Romans 8: 22–23; Philippians 3:20; Revelation 22:3–5). It will be beautiful beyond description (Revelation 21). There will also be meaningful work (Isaiah 65:21–23) without the frustrations and weariness of it.[119] Said Reagan Rose, "In other words, when our Lord makes all

---

119 Reagan Rose, "Will We Work in Heaven?" *Redeeming Productivity,* accessed August 22, 2019. https://www.redeemingproductivity.com/will-we-work-in-heaven/. There is in scripture a distinction between the temporary state of our spirits being with Christ in heaven and when the new heaven and earth are established. At this point in time, we will have glorified bodies, like Jesus did when He rose from the dead. For this purpose of this meditation, we will use the term "heaven" to include both states.

things new, He will abolish every case of the Mondays ... Our work will be restful, enjoyable, and meaningful."[120]

Doesn't this sound like the richest of earthly lives, except without the pain and struggle—the best of life on steroids? Without the impact of sin and brokenness upon us, it will be freedom, love, and joy like we've never experienced before. An old soul, I think I will spend my first hours in heaven laughing out of relief!

What we often don't consider on this side of the veil is that we bring with us into the next life who we have worked with the Master Gardener to become, as well as the effects of our lives. *We* are the result of the Master Gardener's work in our lives— His harvest. Our impact upon others is shown in their lives and stories—our harvest. This is a harvest that weeds will never choke, and death will never claim.

May your harvest in heaven be bountiful!

---

120 Ibid.

5.7 SUSTAINING OUR IMPACT IN THIS WORLD

Throughout this book, we've addressed ways to make meaning. Using the metaphor of dirt, we sought to explain how making meaning is strenuous, requires sacrifice and discipline, and will likely involve some messiness in working with people. We will also be faced with adversity and will need to grow in order to continue making meaning.

We all have had the privilege of experiencing precious instances of richness in life, of deep meaning. But how do we sustain this so that our impact, the harvest, is greater and will occur regularly in our lives? First, we need to develop and *maintain* a character that is filled with love, integrity, empathy, and strength. This isn't easy. Many people start out with good intentions to help others in need but are derailed by character flaws that promote self or exploit others for personal gain. Impacting the world needs to be balanced with self-monitoring of motivation, time spent with family and friends to ground us, and spiritual activities that infuse our motivation and strengthen us internally.

Secondly, we may need additional training. This may involve education in a new profession, or educational sessions that provide knowledge in making meaning through helping others. Some may relish training needed in knowledgeably helping people, but for others, this involves too much effort, particularly when training is ongoing, and they may step back.

Third, we need commitment and consistency. Although some might argue that helping sporadically is better than not helping at all, helping people often requires some consistency. If we involve ourselves with individuals but then pull out shortly after starting our work, some of the benefits of our work may be compromised, those we were working with may be frustrated, and we may become jaded. Here, the "counting the cost" principle that Jesus spoke of is helpful: we need to be careful how thin we spread ourselves and put our hands to do what we have committed to do.

An ongoing impact also requires ongoing discernment. We need to consider the validity of the causes we're involved with, either through physical work or monetary support. For example, do the organizations we support use funds appropriately, or are funds splurged in ways that we deem inappropriate? If we're financially helping people we know personally, are they using these funds wisely? Regular examination of the causes we support is important. Sometimes, given changes in an organization or situation, stepping back from a commitment is prudent. For those who struggle with this, it may be important to realize that we may be called to contribute to a certain work for only a season.

Sustaining our impact in this world demands development and maintenance of character, training, commitment and consistency, as well as discernment. In being cognizant of these important elements in making meaning, we may truly see the harvest over the long term.

AFTERWORD

The information in this book comes from many years of working with people in a variety of settings. We have gathered this carefully, seeking to incorporate these insights into our own lives. However, these understandings have gripped us strongly during these months of writing this book, in the dirt of Annette's Stage Four cancer. We don't know what the future will hold, but we have experienced the Master Gardener's work in our lives and the challenge and grace to trust Him more fully. We trust that there will be good fruit!

Remember "Sally," the lady who didn't know why she was put here on earth (see "Vocation: Meaning in Us; Meaning for the World")? While she doesn't identify her vocation, this lady obviously has a calling to love and serve. She has been involved in prayer ministries in her church, served in a variety of capacities from children's ministries to funeral receptions, and seeks to help people in need in her community; hurting people seek her out. If she doesn't have the resources for them, she involves someone else who does. Her meaningful life has had great impact; her harvest is wonderful.

Perhaps while reading this book you realized that you can make some changes, be more intentional, and live life meaningfully—for yourself, others, and God. Wonderful! Or maybe you're like Sally, never having properly assessed the life you've lived because you didn't value your contributions to the world. We trust you have been affirmed.

In the process of working with the dirt in life, developing a garden that will produce a good crop, may each of us hear the commendation from our Master Gardener:

Well done, good and faithful servant! You have been faithful with a few things; I will put you in charge of many things. Come and share your master's happiness!

—Matthew 25:21